ity

© Alan Edwards

Equity in
Your Coaching

sports coach UK is the brand name of The National Coaching Foundation and has been such since April 2001.

ISBN: 978-1-905540-35-8

Great Coaches...Great Sport

sports coach UK
114 Cardigan Road
Headingley
Leeds LS6 3BJ
Tel: 0113-274 4802 Fax: 0113-275 5019
Email: coaching@sportscoachuk.org
Website: www.sportscoachuk.org

First Edition
Developed from an original text by Annie Kerr in conjunction with Michelle-Vernon Way and Warwick Andrews.

Second Edition
Revised by Simon Kirkland

The publishers would like to thank the following for their valuable input to this handbook: Andy Brittles (English Federation of Disability Sport), Liz Davidson (Women's Sports Foundation), Steve McQuaid and Heather Moir (sports coach UK), Novlette Rennie (Sporting Equals), Sports Council for Northern Ireland, Sports Council for Wales, Sport England, **sport**scotland and UK Sport.

Cover photos courtesy of Alan Edwards and www.actionplus.co.uk

All photos courtesy of sports coach UK unless otherwise stated.

Published on behalf of **sports coach UK** by

Coachwise 1st4sport

Coachwise Business Solutions
Chelsea Close
Off Amberley Road
Armley
Leeds LS12 4HP
Tel: 0113-231 1310
Fax: 0113-231 9606
Email: enquiries@coachwisesolutions.co.uk
Website: www.coachwisesolutions.co.uk

Throughout this resource, the pronouns he, she, him, her and so on are interchangeable and intended to be inclusive of both males and females.

sports coach UK will ensure that it has professional and ethical values and that all its practices are inclusive and equitable.

081034

Preface

Think back to the first time you participated in your sport. Imagine if your coach had said that you couldn't participate because you had a disability. What if your coach had insisted you wear specific sports clothing, but, for religious reasons, you couldn't and, therefore, wouldn't have been able to take part? Or if your team or coach insisted that you change in another room because of your sexuality, or if your coach said girls are no good at sport. How would this have made you feel? It's certainly unlikely that you would have been able to progress to the stage you're at in your sport today.

Coaching is, first and foremost, about people – encouraging them to enjoy the positive benefits of sport and helping them to achieve their potential. Everyone should have access to sport, regardless of ability, ethnic group, gender, age, background or sexuality. Although we may like to think this is the case, in reality, it is not. Research has shown that many groups of people are under-represented in all areas of sport, including coaching. For example, between the Moscow Olympics in 1980 and the Sydney Olympics in 2000, the proportion of female coaches in the British team fell from 9% to 7.6%, despite the rise in the number of female athletes competing. However, at the Athens Olympics in 2004, although 39% of athletes were women, still only 10% of coaches were women. From the 'Sports Coaching in the UK Report' conducted in 2004, coaches were predominantly white, male and middle class[1].

Everyone involved in sport has a responsibility to improve this situation – as a coach, you have an important role to play. Sports equity and being equitable mean ensuring your coaching sessions are fair, open and accessible to everyone who wants to take part. This might seem a daunting prospect, but don't worry. It doesn't mean having to learn a whole new set of coaching skills; it's more about applying and extending your existing skills and experience to meet the needs of present and potential participants. *Equity in Your Coaching* will help you do this.

Although many different groups of people are disadvantaged in sport, this resource will focus on groups who generally experience discrimination on a more regular basis, not only in sport, but in their daily lives:

• Disabled people

• People from ethnic minorities

• Women and girls

• People from economically disadvantaged backgrounds

• People of different ages

• Gay, lesbian, bisexual and transgender people.

These are referred to as key target groups.

---

[1] Taken from Mori (2004) 'Sports Coaching in the UK Final Report', www.sportscoachuk.org/NR/rdonlyres/4CC9B752-610A-4060-895E-D6C7BDEDCAB9/0/SportsCoachingUKFinalReport.pdf

The aim is not to judge or criticise your coaching practice or opinions, but to raise your awareness of equity issues and help you identify ways of becoming a more equitable coach. By adopting the principles highlighted in this resource, you will help to make your sport enjoyable and accessible to all sections of society, and hopefully attract new participants to your coaching sessions.

Each section of the resource provides information, activities and questions to help you check your understanding and apply it to your own coaching. By the end of the resource, you should be able to:

- explain what sports equity, equal opportunities and equality mean and why they are important
- identify barriers that may prevent the key target groups from participating in sport
- overcome the barriers that may prevent the key target groups from participating in sport
- be aware of the appropriate language and terminology to use when referring to the key target groups
- challenge inequitable behaviour during your coaching sessions
- interpret the legal framework that affects coaching
- develop an equity action plan
- know who to contact for additional information relating to coaching the key target groups.

The resource supports a three-hour sports coach UK workshop which you are strongly recommended to attend. This will help you to put the theory behind equity into practice and apply it to your own coaching. All coaches are offered access to support and advice after the workshop. Workshop dates and locations are available from the sports coach UK Workshop Booking Centre (see page 128 for contact details).

Contents

Section 4 – Tips for More Equitable Coaching

Section 5 – Challenging Inequitable Behaviour

Section 6 – Legal Framework Affecting Equity

Section 7 – Action Plan for Change

Section 8 – Where Next?

Appendices

© Alan Edwards

Section 1

Setting the Context

1.0 What's In It For You?

The aim of this resource is to help you apply and enhance your existing skills and experience to make your coaching sessions accessible to all members of the community. Before exploring exactly how to do this, it is important that you understand the concepts of sports equity, equal opportunities and equality, and why they are so important. The terms are used in general language, but are not often defined and explained in sporting and coaching contexts. However, this section will provide you with useful background information and help you to understand that equality in sport is not simply about making sport more politically correct, but about improving sporting opportunities for everyone, while making sure everyone is treated fairly.

By the end of the section, you should be able to explain:

• what sports equity, equal opportunities and equality mean, and the differences between them

• which groups of people are regularly disadvantaged in sport

• why sports equity is important.

1.1 What do Sports Equity, Equal Opportunities and Equality Mean?

Points of interest

> *Sports equity is about fairness in sport, equality of access, recognising inequalities and taking steps to address them. It is about changing the culture and structure of sport to ensure that it becomes equally accessible to everyone in society.*
>
> Sport England, 2000[1]

Achieving sports equity depends on everybody involved in sport:

- recognising that certain groups of people are disadvantaged[2] and may, therefore, be discriminated[3] against because of their gender, age, race, disability, faith or sexual orientation, not just in sport, but in society in general
- treating everyone equally, but recognising that some groups of people have different needs
- sharing resources and making sport accessible to disadvantaged groups of people.

Equal Opportunities

Equal opportunities is about the law and how it is applied in the workplace. The law only intervenes when it is clear that legislation is the only way to deal with discriminative acts. Therefore, equal opportunities is about ensuring employment practices are fair and that the workplace is an environment free from discrimination and harassment. Employers are required to comply with UK and EU discrimination legislation.

Equality

Equality is the state of being equal – treating individuals equally, which does not necessarily mean treating them the same. In some cases, the need for equality may require unequal effort, to ensure that the principle of equality is achieved.

1.2 Who is Disadvantaged in Sport?

Everyone is treated unfairly in some way at times – no doubt you can think of a few occasions when you've been on the receiving end of unfair treatment. The following activity asks you to think of an example based on your own experiences.

ACTIVITY 1

Think of an incident, not necessarily in sport, when you felt you were treated unfairly. Make a brief note of the incident in the space provided below and answer the questions that follow on page 3.

---

1   Sport England (2000) *Making English Sport Inclusive: Equity Guidelines for Governing Bodies.* London: Sport England. Ref no: SE/1043/1M/6/00

2 and 3 For a definition of this and other terms associated with sports equity, see Appendix A.

Why do you think you were treated unfairly?

How did this make you feel?

What effect did it have on you?

What did you do about it?

Now, compare your experience as a coach with those described in the following scenarios:

Scenario 1

Tariq is a wheelchair user and a coach at a local table tennis club. The club has had a very successful season and is in a good position to win the league, with Tariq being an important member of the coaching team. The head coach wants to move the training sessions to what he feels is a better venue, nearer to where he lives. However, this venue is not accessible to wheelchairs – there are no parking facilities, no ramp up to the main entrance, only steps, and the changing rooms are very small and cramped.

Scenario 2

Palvinda is Asian and has been a member of her local netball club for some time. She has recently been selected for the club team and will be competing regularly in local and regional tournaments. Her coach insists that all team members wear the official team kit during training sessions and at all competitions. However, this includes a sports skirt, which Palvinda cannot wear for religious reasons – she usually wears tracksuit bottoms instead.

Scenario 3

Jackie is an avid squash player and has been top of the women's squash ladder at her local club for several months. To make things more challenging and improve her game further, she asks if she can join the men's squash ladder instead. However, the club chair says that this is against club regulations and that the men wouldn't think she was good enough to play.

Scenario 4

Tracey has been a youth coach for 20 years and has coached a number of successful teams, as well as developing a number of players who have continued playing after they have left her teams. Tracey has applied for the position of county youth coach, which is a paid position. She later discovers that the position is given to a coach who has the same qualifications, but who is 15 years younger and lacks the experience she possesses.

Scenario 5

Kerry always turns up late to training sessions. The coach drops her from the squad after she is late for the third consecutive session. She is a carer for her mother and is unable to get a lift by car or afford a taxi to the coaching session, like the other participants. She has to wait for a bus, so she is unable to get to the coaching session on time.

Scenario 6

Steve plays for his hockey team and mentioned to the captain that he is going to the club Christmas party with his partner, Peter. The captain informs Steve that the party is for female partners only, and following this, Steve is asked to change at home before coming to training or matches.

Tariq, Palvinda, Jackie, Tracey, Kerry and Steve all have something in common – they've all been treated unfairly in their sport:

- Tariq feels that, by suggesting the club venue is moved, the head coach is acting unfairly. Although probably not intending to discriminate against Tariq, he has failed to realise how difficult it will make things for him. It'll be harder for Tariq to get to the venue and, once he's there, it will be difficult for him to get into the building itself, as well as make use of the changing facilities.

- Palvinda feels that her coach is acting unreasonably, insisting that she wears a sports skirt, particularly as wearing tracksuit bottoms instead would pose no threat to her safety.

- Jackie feels that she is being discriminated against because she is a woman. She is annoyed that the club chair assumes the men will think she's not good enough to play against them and that he refuses to consider reviewing club regulations or giving her the opportunity to prove her ability.

- Tracey feels that she has been discriminated against because of her age. She is disappointed that the county committee felt that a younger person with less experience could do the job better, as this is a position Tracey has been aiming for, to further improve her coaching and seek the opportunity to move on to the next level of coach education.

- Kerry feels that she is being treated unfairly as she does not have the ability of other participants to get to sessions on time, as her family cannot afford a car or a taxi to get her to the session. She is disappointed and frustrated as she always works very hard in training sessions, and always competes well in competitions.

- Steve feels very unfairly treated as he cannot bring his long-standing partner to the Christmas party, and has to change in another changing room or at home before playing the sport he loves.

Although many different groups of people are disadvantaged in sport, Tariq, Palvinda, Jackie, Tracey, Kerry and Steve each belong to particular groups of people who generally experience discrimination on a more regular basis, not only in sport, but in their daily lives:

Points of interest

- Disabled people
- People from ethnic minorities
- Women and girls
- Economically disadvantaged people
- People of different ages
- Gay, lesbian, bisexual and transgender people

This resource will focus on these groups. From now on, the term 'key target groups' will be used when referring to them collectively.

Remember!

- For ease of reference, the guidance in this resource is often divided into separate sections for each of the key target groups. However, this doesn't mean that each group should be treated in isolation. Remember, some of the people you coach may belong to a combination of groups (eg Asian women, disabled participants from ethnic minorities), so it's important to understand the needs of **all** the key target groups.

- Although this resource concentrates on these key target groups, remember that these aren't the only ones, and that other groups of people may be disadvantaged in your sport. It's important to identify who these people are and to seek specific advice from appropriate sources.

© www.actionplus.co.uk

1.3 Why is Sports Equity Important?

Think back to the main elements of the sports equity definition introduced on page 2, where it was identified that inequalities need to be identified before action can be taken.

Recognising Inequalities

National Population

Society should be reflected in sport. For example, the 2001 Census revealed that the national population included:

- 51.4% women
- 5% disabled people
- 10% people from ethnic minorities.

Sports Participation in the UK

However, a survey[1] carried out by the Office of National Statistics, on behalf of Sport England, revealed that the overall participation rate for:

• ethnic minority groups is 40%, compared with a national average of 46%
• men from ethnic minorities is 49%, compared with a national average of 54%
• women from ethnic minorities is 32%, compared with a national average of 39%.

The findings of the survey also concluded that the picture is much more complex than simply looking at participation rates suggests, as there is considerable variation in the levels of participation between:

• men and women
• different ethnic groups
• different sports.

For example, on average, the participation rates for Black Caribbean (39%), Indian (39%) and, in particular, Pakistani (31%) and Bangladeshi (30%) populations, are below the national average (46%). Only the participation rate for the Black Other group (60%) is higher than the national average.

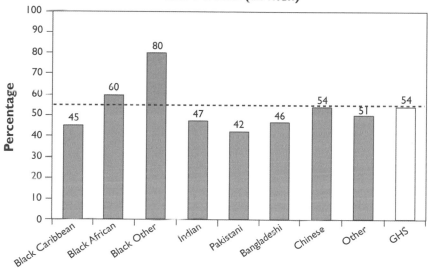

Participation in at least one activity (excluding walking) over the last 4 weeks (all men)

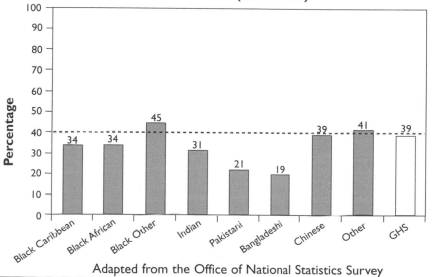

Participation in at least one activity (excluding walking) over the last 4 weeks (all women)

Adapted from the Office of National Statistics Survey

---

[1] Rowe, N and Champion, R (2000) *Sports Participation and Ethnicity in England: National Survey 1999/2000 Headline Findings.* London: Sport England. Ref no: SE/1073

The survey also recognised that, in some sports, participation rates for ethnic minority groups are relatively high.

In 2002, Sport England integrated the results of the General Household Survey and the Young People's Sports Survey for England, and produced the Sports Equity Index. The Sports Equity Index has been formulated to provide the evidence base for sports equity policy and initiatives in England, and was devised to:

• assist all those involved in sports development to better understand the levels of inequality that currently exist in sports participation

• provide the evidence base for determining policy priorities, setting targets and measuring achievements.

In Scotland, surveys of attitudes found some interesting perceptions about sport. In all but the youngest age groups, people from ethnic minorities participate in sport and physical education less frequently than white people of the same age: 60%, compared to 74%, in the 25–34 age group; 51%, compared to 69%, in the 34–44 age group, and 33%, versus 63%, in the 45–54 age group.

'That's something that Western people do' – some people from ethnic minorities feel that they simply won't fit in and that ethnic minorities don't do sport.

An estimated 6%[1] of the population of England is lesbian, gay, bisexual or transgender (LGBT); however, it is difficult to identify LGBT role models in sport. In some sports, it appears to be accepted that women are openly lesbian, but men appear not to be accepted if they are gay. This is particularly the case in team sports. However, in other areas of society, this appears to be reversed. In dance, for example, it appears that gay men are accepted, yet being lesbian appears to be frowned upon.

Active People

According to the Active People survey carried out in 2006, swimming is the most popular activity for women, followed by gym-based exercise. Tennis and badminton both appear in the top 10 and the top team sport is football. 1% of the post-16 female population play football.

This Active People Survey (Oct 2005–Oct 2006), carried out by Sport England, captured data from 363,724 adult (16+) participants in England by telephone interview. At least 1000 interviews were conducted per local authority, except for the City of London, Isles of Scilly and Birmingham. Data was captured on type, duration and intensity of people's participation in different kinds of sport and active recreation. Information was also collected regarding volunteering, club membership, tuition, competitive sport and satisfaction with local club provision.

Active People Survey

KPI 1: At least 3 days a week x 30 minutes moderate participation[2]	
Variable	England
All adults	21%
Male	23.7%
Female	18.5%
White	21.2%
Non-white	18.6%

KPI 2: At least 1 hour a week of volunteering to support sport[2]	
Variable	England
All adults	4.7%
Male	6.1%
Female	3.4%
White	4.8%
Non-white	3.6%

[1] Source of statistics: Sport England (2000) *Making English Sport Inclusive: Equity Guidelines for Governing Bodies*. London: Sport England. Ref no: SE/1043/1M/6/00

[2] The tables are adapted from the Sport England Active People Survey 2006. The definitions (variables) are taken from those identified by the survey company.

UK Coaching Profiles

A similarly complex picture is painted when you look at coaching, as illustrated in the examples below:

• There are very few female coaches from any section of society at an elite level.

• Between the Moscow Olympics in 1980 and the Sydney Olympics in 2000, the proportion of female coaches within the British team fell from 9% to 7.6%, despite the rise in the number of female athletes competing to over 40%. However, at the Athens Olympics in 2004, the proportion did rise to 10%.

• In terms of female participants from ethnic minorities at the Olympics, it is easy to think of some high-profile black female athletes (eg Denise Lewis or Dame Kelly Holmes). However, it is much more difficult to think of any high-profile black female coaches.

• There are very few disabled coaches and there is an assumption that the ones there are can only coach disabled participants.

Sports Coaching in the UK Final Report (sports coach UK/Mori, 2004)

Men are much more likely to be involved in sports coaching than women, with three-quarters (76%) of those currently coaching being male (c.930,000 men compared with c.300,000 women). In addition, significantly more men than women have coached in the past but no longer coach, and almost three times as many men than women would like to take up coaching in the future.

Similar to patterns in sports participation, the proportion of the population who are currently coaching declines with age. Four per cent of adults aged under 25 are involved in sports coaching, compared with only one per cent of those aged over 55 (c.290,000 v c.160,000 people respectively). Outside these age groups, the proportion of coaches remains very similar across the age bands – with around 3.0% of 25-55 year olds (c.780,000) currently coaching.

Interestingly, the number of lapsed coaches is not significantly affected by age. Indeed, more young people are lapsed coaches than the older age group (7.8% of 15-24 year olds versus 6.7% of those aged 55+). Coach retention is clearly an issue that needs to be addressed across all age bands.

ABC1s represent around half of the adult population of the UK, but almost seven in ten of the UK's sports coaches (c.850,000 coaches are ABC1s compared with only c.380,000 C2DEs).

People of White origin appear more likely to be sports coaches than those from Black and minority ethnic groups (BMEs). (However, this finding should be treated with caution, as the difference falls outside the boundaries of statistical reliability.)

However, BMEs are significantly more likely to be interested in becoming sports coaches, than those of a White ethnic origin. This may indicate that there are barriers which need to be overcome to ensure greater involvement in sports coaching among BMEs in the future.

Local Demographics

It is important to recognise that certain groups of people may be excluded from your sport, whether intentionally or not. Use national population statistics as a general guide to gauge how equitable your coaching sessions are. However, remember that they only reflect the national average, and that you also need to bear in mind the huge regional/local variations that can occur. For example, in 1996, the ethnic minority population in London was 26%, in the West Midlands 10% and in the South West 1%[1].

---

[1] Source of statistics: Sport England (2000) *Making English Sport Inclusive: Equity Guidelines for Governing Bodies*. London: Sport England. Ref no: SE/1043/1M/6/00

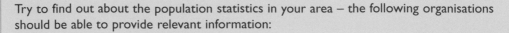

Try to find out about the population statistics in your area – the following organisations should be able to provide relevant information:

• Local council
• General Register Office for Scotland
• Northern Ireland Statistics and Research Agency
• Office for National Statistics (England and Wales).

1.4 Legal Requirements

Providing sporting opportunities for everyone in society, regardless of their ability, ethnic group, gender, age, background or sexuality, is not just a moral responsibility, but could also be a legal requirement in some instances, particularly for organisations deemed to be service providers (eg local authorities, governing bodies of sport, sporting organisations).

By delivering coaching sessions, you are providing a service, but this does not necessarily classify you as the service provider in the eyes of the law. If you are employed by another party (eg a sports club), your employer is ultimately responsible for your actions. More often than not, it is the employer, not the employee, who is cited in employment tribunal/court cases. However, this should not be used as an excuse for inequitable practice on your part. You still have an important role to play in helping your employer respond positively to equity legislation and other equity-related initiatives. You may find yourself being asked to ensure that, where possible, your coaching sessions are open and accessible to all sections of the community.

On the other hand, you may be one of the many coaches who work on a voluntary basis in a wide variety of situations and who receive little or no payment for their services and expertise, and little advice and support. Although the service you provide may not be subject to the same legal requirements as that of official service providers, it is still essential that your coaching sessions are as equitable as possible and that they reflect best practice at all times.

It is important to understand the legal context so as a coach, you do not act inequitably.

Section Six will explore the potential sources of liability that may affect you; this section will describe the main equal opportunities legislation.

The descriptions below do not give a full statement of law and are not a substitute for professional advice. These are the key anti-discriminatory laws in the UK:

• Equal Pay Act 1970 Equal Value (Amendment) Regulations 1983
• Rehabilitation of Offenders Act 1974
• Sex Discrimination Act 1975, 1986 and 1999
• Race Relations Act 1976, Amendment Act 2000
• Employment Protection (Consolidation) Act 1978
• Children Act 1989 and 2004
• Disability Discrimination Act 1995 and 2004
• Race Relations (Northern Ireland) Order 1997
• Northern Ireland Act 1998
• Scotland Act 1998
• Human Rights Act 1998
• Employment Equality (Sexual Orientation) Regulations 2003
• Employment Equality (Religion and Belief) Regulations 2003
• Disability Discrimination Act 2005

• Equality Act 2006

• Employment Equality (Age) Regulations 2006

Equal Pay Act 1970 Equal Value (Amendment) Regulations 1983

The Act requires equal treatment for women (and men) in pay and other contractual conditions of service. A woman only has to show that she is doing like, equivalent or equal value of work to a man.

Women and men are entitled to equal pay and conditions if:

• they are employed on like work, which means that their work is the same or broadly similar

• their jobs have been given equivalent rating under a non-discriminatory job evaluation scheme

• their work is of equal value, in terms of effort, skill, decision making or other demands.

Rehabilitation of Offenders Act 1974

The Act enables some criminal convictions to become 'spent' or ignored, after a 'rehabilitation period'. A rehabilitation period is a set length of time from the date of conviction. After this period, with certain exceptions, an ex-offender is not normally obliged to mention the conviction when applying for a job or insurance. Exceptions to the Act, where people will be expected to declare convictions even if they are spent, include appointment to any post providing care/schooling/training/supervision to people under the age of 18, or vulnerable adults. Criminal-record checks will reveal both spent and unspent convictions.

Sex Discrimination Act 1975, 1986 and 1999

The Act makes it unlawful to discriminate directly or indirectly on the grounds of a person's sex and marital status (the 1999 amendment includes gender reassignment). It is unlawful for employers to discriminate in recruitment, promotion, training and transfer, terms and conditions of employment, and dismissal.

Race Relations Act 1976 and Race Relations (Amendment) Act 2000

The Act makes it unlawful to discriminate directly or indirectly on the grounds of a person's colour, race, nationality, ethnic or national origin. It is unlawful for employers to discriminate in recruitment, promotion, training and transfer, terms and conditions of employment, and dismissal. The 2000 amendment put public authorities under a statutory duty to promote race equality (in light of the findings of the Stephen Lawrence inquiry).

> **Liability**
>
> Employers can be held accountable for the action of their employees in the first instance. This means that, even if an employer would not encourage or sanction acts of discrimination, it is still liable for any discriminatory acts committed by its employees.
>
> Employers do have a legal defence available to them, which is that they have 'taken such steps as were reasonably practicable, to prevent the employee from committing a discriminatory act' (Race Relations Act and Sex Discrimination Act).

Unlawful discrimination under the Race Relations Act and Sex Discrimination Act includes:

• **direct discrimination** – consists of treating a person less favourably than others on the grounds of sex or race

• **indirect discrimination** – consists of applying a requirement or condition which, whether intentional or not, adversely affects one group rather than another

• **harassment** – may be on grounds of sex, race, disability, sexuality or sexual status. It is necessary to show that harassment amounts to 'detriment' to the victim.

Employment Protection (Consolidation) Act 1978

The Act provides the statutory maternity rights scheme. Under this provision, employers are required to make statutory maternity payments to women employees who have to go on maternity leave.

These rights allow the woman employee to return to the same job or suitable alternative work after the maternity period. The Act ensures that women on maternity leave cannot be made redundant.

Children Act 1989 and 2004

This Act has reformed the law relating to children and has brought together public and private law about children.

Disability Discrimination Act (DDA) 1995 and 2004

It is unlawful for an employer with 15 or more employees (including part-time, temporary workers and people with fixed-term contracts) to discriminate against current or prospective employees.

Discrimination occurs when an employee or job applicant receives less favourable treatment or is denied equal opportunities because she is disabled, and the treatment cannot be justified.

It is unlawful for a provider of goods, services or facilities to discriminate against a disabled person:

• in refusing to provide or deliberately not providing goods, services or facilities that are normally provided to members of the public
• in offering a lower standard of goods, services and facilities
• in terms of the goods, services and facilities provided.

Since October 2004, the new code of practice covering Part III of the Disability Discrimination Act (DDA) 1995 has been in force.

The new code of practice encourages service providers not to wait until a disabled person brings a 'barrier' to their attention in order to make a reasonable adjustment. Sports clubs should seek compliance with the DDA 1995 Part III, which relates to 'service providers' and states: 'A service provider discriminates against a disabled person if, for a reason related to a person's disability, the service provider treats that person less favourably than they would treat others, and the service provider cannot demonstrate that the less favourable treatment is justified.'

In practice, this means that service providers can discriminate against a disabled person by:

• refusing to provide a service
• offering a worse standard of service
• offering a service on worse terms
• failing to comply with their duty to make reasonable adjustments.

Disability Rights Commission Act 1999

This Act led to the establishment of the Disability Rights Commission (DRC) in April 2000, and sets out the DRC's statutory duties:

• to work to eliminate discrimination against disabled people
• to promote equal opportunities for disabled people
• to encourage good practice in the treatment of disabled people
• to advise the government on the working of disability legislation.

Human Rights Act 1998

The Act has been effective since October 2000 and has implications for workplace issues such as harassment, religious tolerance and gay rights. Also included in the Act are the rights to a hearing and representation.

Employment Equality (Sexual Orientation) Regulations 2003
Employment Equality (Religion and Belief) Regulations 2003

This Regulation outlaws discrimination in employment and vocational training on the grounds of sexual orientation, religion and belief. It also outlaws direct and indirect discrimination, harassment and victimisation.

Disability Discrimination Act (DDA) 2005

In April 2005, a new Disability Discrimination Act was passed by Parliament, which amends or extends existing provisions in the DDA 1995, including:

• making it unlawful for operators of transport vehicles to discriminate against disabled people

• making it easier for disabled people to rent property and for tenants to make disability-related adaptations

• making sure that private clubs with 25 or more members cannot keep disabled people out, just because they have a disability

• extending protection to cover people who have HIV, cancer and multiple sclerosis from the moment they are diagnosed

• ensuring that discrimination law covers all the activities of the public sector

• requiring public bodies to promote equality of opportunity for disabled people.

www.direct.gov.uk/en/DisabledPeople/RightsAndObligations/DisabilityRights/DG 4001068

Equality Act 2006

This Act was devised to make provision for the establishment of the Commission for Equality and Human Rights, to dissolve the Equal Opportunities Commission, the Commission for Racial Equality and the Disability Rights Commission, to make provision about discrimination on grounds of religion or belief, to enable provision to be made about discrimination on grounds of sexual orientation, to impose duties relating to sex discrimination on persons performing public functions, and to amend the Disability Discrimination Act 1995.

General Duty of the Commission for Equality and Human Rights

The Commission shall exercise its functions under this Part with a view to encouraging and supporting the development of a society in which:

(a) people's ability to achieve their potential is not limited by prejudice or discrimination

(b) there is respect for, and protection of, each individual's human rights

(c) there is respect for the dignity and worth of each individual

(d) each individual has an equal opportunity to participate in society

(e) there is mutual respect between groups, based on understanding and valuing diversity, and on shared respect for equality and human rights.

Points of interest

Code of Practice for Sports Coaches

sports coach UK has developed a *Code of Practice for Sports Coaches* in order to establish, publicise and maintain standards of ethical behaviour in coaching practice, and to inform and protect members of the public using the services of sports coaches. The Code forms the Values Statement underpinning the National Occupational Standards for Coaching, Teaching and Instructing reviewed in 2004, led by SkillsActive.

The Code states that:

Coaches must respect the rights, dignity and worth of every human being and their ultimate right to self-determination. Specifically, coaches must treat everyone equitably and sensitively, within the context of their activity and ability, regardless of gender, ethnic origin, cultural background, sexual orientation, religion or political affiliation.

sports coach UK Code of Practice for Sports Coaches (2005)

The status of the coach continues to increase in the perception of the public at large, so it is therefore crucial for you to adopt and abide by the Code, which reflects the highest standards of good coaching practice. In doing so, you accept your responsibility to:

- sports participants and their parents/families
- coaching and other colleagues
- your governing body
- your coaching employer
- society.

Employment Equality (Age) Regulations 2006

This Regulation outlaws discrimination in employment and vocational training on the grounds of age. It also outlaws direct and indirect discrimination, harassment and victimisation.

The government has recognised the value of sport in promoting the inclusion of all groups of people in society, and as part of programmes to reduce crime and antisocial behaviour. Its agenda in relation to equity in society in general also applies to sport. As a result, many initiatives and organisations have been introduced to improve the sporting opportunities available to the key target groups.

Appendix B provides a summary of the key organisations and initiatives you should be aware of. It is divided into the following four sections:

- Government Agenda takes a look at key government initiatives designed to provide better sporting opportunities for the key target groups.
- Sports Agenda examines the progress made by key UK sports organisations.
- Coaching Agenda looks at coaching-specific initiatives.
- Equality Agenda looks at equality agendas across the UK.

To obtain a copy of the Code, and for further information about sports coach UK membership services, contact Coachwise 1st4sport (see page 128 for contact details).

Appendix B will help you look beyond government policy to see the bigger picture and understand why sports equity in coaching is so important.

1.5 Summary

This section should have helped you to understand the concept of sports equity and why it is so important. The key points you need to remember are listed in the panel below.

- The key element of sports equity is **recognising inequalities** (acknowledging that certain groups of people are under-represented in all areas of sport). Understanding people's background's will assist you in planning more effective coaching sessions.

- Many different groups of people are disadvantaged in sport. This will vary across the country and to which group. However, some groups experience discrimination on a more regular basis, not only in sport, but in their daily lives. This resource will therefore focus on the following key target groups:
  - disabled people
  - people from ethnic minorities
  - women and girls
  - people from economically disadvantaged backgrounds
  - people of different ages
  - gay, lesbian, bisexual and transgender people.

- Providing sporting opportunities for everyone, regardless of ability, ethnic group, gender, age, background or sexuality, is not just a moral duty, it is also a legal requirement. The Acts of Parliament you particularly need to be aware of are:

  - Equal Pay Act 1970 Equal Value (Amendment) Regulations 1983
  - Rehabilitation of Offenders Act 1974
  - Sex Discrimination Act 1975, 1986 and 1999
  - Race Relations Act 1976, Amendment Act 2000
  - Employment Protection (Consolidation) Act 1978
  - Children Act 1989 and 2004
  - Disability Discrimination Act 1995 and 2004
  - Race Relations (Northern Ireland) Order 1997
  - Northern Ireland Act 1998
  - Scotland Act 1998
  - Human Rights Act 1998
  - Employment Equality (Sexual Orientation) Regulations 2003
  - Employment Equality (Religion and Belief) Regulations 2003
  - Disability Discrimination Act 2005
  - Equality Act 2006
  - Employment Equality (Age) Regulations 2006

- Ensuring your coaching sessions are as accessible as possible means encouraging the key target groups to attend. To do this, it is important to understand why they might be put off from doing so. Section Two looks at the barriers that may prevent the key target groups from participating in sport.

16

Section 2

Barriers to Participation

2.0 What's In It For You?

There are a variety of reasons why people could be put off from attending your coaching sessions. This could be down to something either within or beyond your control. To ensure your coaching sessions are as accessible as possible, it is important to understand the barriers that might prevent the key target groups from participating.

Some barriers to participation apply to everyone, not just people from the key target groups. These include things like:

• lack of awareness of sports activities on offer, due to poor marketing and promotion

• inconvenient times

• lack of spare time

• domestic/work commitments taking priority

• inconvenient venues

• poor facilities

• lack of transport

• fear for personal safety getting to and from the venue

• expense of participation

• previous negative experiences (eg bad memories of PE lessons at school)

• lack of motivation

• parental attitudes and influences.

However, some barriers are particularly relevant to people from the key target groups. This section is divided into subsections which deal with each of the key target groups in turn. By the end of the section, you should be able to:

• explain the barriers to participation for each key target group

• identify the barriers to participation in specific coaching scenarios.

2.1 Disabled People

The following panel identifies the key issues that may act as barriers to disabled people participating in sport.

BARRIERS TO PARTICIPATION IN SPORT

Assumptions

- Assumption that disabled people only take part in sport for therapeutic reasons. However, many take part for the same reasons as non-disabled people.
- Assumptions about which sports disabled people are interested in.
- Assumptions about which sports disabled people can and cannot participate in.
- Assumptions about what disabled people can and cannot do.
- Assumption that disabled people can't be integrated into coaching sessions for non-disabled people, and that separate sessions need to be provided.
- Assumption that disabled people are only in wheelchairs.

Lack of Informed Coaches

- Lack of coaches who are appropriately trained and informed about coaching disabled people.
- Lack of understanding among coaches about the different needs of different impairment groups.
- Lack of competitive opportunities.

Poor Communication

- This includes failure to:
  - consult directly with disabled people to find out about their needs and aspirations
  - advertise sports opportunities for disabled people adequately and appropriately, and in places they regularly go to (eg day centres, special schools, youth clubs)
  - provide adequate encouragement – some disabled people have low self-esteem and need more than just an advertisement to encourage them to take part in sport.
- Use of inappropriate language.

Poor Facilities

- Lack of access to and within venues.
- Inadequate changing facilities.
- Lack of specialist equipment.

Poor Timing

- Specialist coaching sessions run at inconvenient times (eg off-peak).

The following scenarios describe two different coaching situations. As you read through them, try to identify whether the organisation/coach could have done more to make the coaching sessions more accessible to disabled people.

Scenario 7

A local voluntary organisation wants to hold a *Come and Try It!* sports day for disabled people. They choose a venue because it is relatively cheap to hire for the day, although it is a bit out of the way on the outskirts of town and isn't on any major bus routes. They ask local sports clubs to hold hourly coaching sessions in their sport for any disabled people that turn up to the session.

The organisation sends letters to local schools and colleges, inviting disabled pupils to come to the *Come and Try It!* day and have a go at some of the activities on offer.

Stop and consider

Do you think the organisation would attract many disabled people to the *Come and Try It* day? Why?

Scenario 8

A local leisure centre runs a judo club for young people every Tuesday evening. The club is both popular and successful, with many members doing well at local competitions.

Most of the club members attend a local school, where there are a number of disabled pupils. Several of the disabled pupils are keen to join the club, but because it is so popular, there are no places left for new members, with or without disabilities.

The club coach therefore starts up a second club night at the leisure centre and divides the new and existing members between the two nights according to level of ability, not disability. Realising that she will need help to run both club nights, she contacts members of the senior judo club to find out if anyone is interested in getting involved in coaching. She plans to encourage any coaches who come forward to work towards the British Judo Association Preliminary Club Coach Award (if they've not already got it) and to attend the sports coach UK workshop 'Coaching Disabled Performers'.

Stop and consider

Do you think the judo coach would succeed in making her club accessible to disabled people? Why?

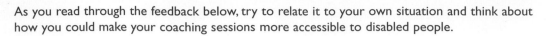

As you read through the feedback below, try to relate it to your own situation and think about how you could make your coaching sessions more accessible to disabled people.

Scenario 7

The organisation would have been unlikely to attract many disabled people to the *Come and Try It!* day for the following reasons:

- Many people who were invited to the event might have been fed up with this kind of *Come and Try It!* day and would have preferred the opportunity to become a member of a sports club.

- Cost took priority over accessibility when the venue for the *Come and Try It!* day was selected. Because of this, it wasn't very easy for people to get to, which explains why attendance was far lower than expected.

- Not only was the venue difficult to get to in the first place, the building itself may not have catered particularly well for people with disabilities. For example:

  – no car park nearby

  – poor access and facilities for people in wheelchairs

  – no hearing induction loops.

- Given the choice, the disabled pupils might have preferred to try different sports to those on offer.

- The organisers and coaches might not have been sufficiently trained or informed about coaching disabled people and, therefore, didn't take into account the different needs of different impairment groups.

- Appropriate equipment may not have been available.

Had the voluntary organisation consulted all the parties involved in the *Come and Try It!* day, prior to making definite arrangements, many of the problems listed above could have been avoided.

Scenario 8

The judo coach would have been likely to succeed in making her club accessible to disabled people for the following reasons:

- She arranged an additional club night, rather than just saying the club was full and couldn't accommodate any new members.

- She divided new and existing members between the two club nights by ability, not disability, rather than running separate club nights for non-disabled and disabled members.

- She contacted the senior judo club to identify potential new coaches to help her run the two club nights. Increasing the number of coaches at the club night would mean that the coach-participant ratio is lower, and that members will receive more individual attention.

- She planned to help senior judo club members work towards a recognised coaching award in judo. This would ensure that all the club's coaches operate in line with the recommended good practice advocated by the British Judo Association.

- She planned to arrange for all club coaches to receive training on coaching disabled people. This would ensure that they understand the needs of the club members who are disabled and that they are able to adapt their coaching methods to support them.

> **Points of interest**
> The coach in Scenario 8 took positive steps to provide sporting opportunities for disabled people. The contrast with Scenario 7 should help you to appreciate just how important it is to be equitable in your coaching.

2.2 People from Ethnic Minorities

The following panel identifies the key issues that may act as barriers to people from ethnic minorities participating in sport.

BARRIERS TO PARTICIPATION IN SPORT

Cultural/Religious Influences

• Religious beliefs – for example, it may not be possible to:

   – wear specified sports kit

   – attend coaching sessions during religious festivals or at times reserved for prayer.

(See Appendix C for further information about religious festivals).

• Lack of single-gender coaching sessions with coach of appropriate gender.

• Lack of privacy in changing areas.

• Lack of parental support – Asian girls, in particular, may experience stricter parental control, which prevents them from participating in out-of-home leisure activities.

• Sport is often viewed as a *luxury* pastime, with little relevance to everyday life.

Fear of Discrimination

• Fear of being stereotyped and discriminated against – people from ethnic minorities are often stereotyped as only being able to play certain sports.

• Fear of racial abuse or attacks.

Low Self-esteem

• Lack of confidence and feeling self-conscious.

• Negative past experiences (eg at school).

• Having no-one to go with.

• Lack of positive images and role models.

Poor Communication

• Use of inappropriate language.

• Inadequate advertising of sports activities available in appropriate places (eg community centres).

Practicalities

• Cost.

• Lack of time.

• Lack of transport.

Unwelcoming Environment at Sports Centre

• Sports facilities often seen as *mainstream* (ie for white communities).

• A feeling of not belonging.

• Unsympathetic staff.

• Language barriers.

The following scenarios describe two different coaching situations. As you read through them, try to identify whether the coaches could have done more to make their coaching sessions more accessible to people from ethnic minorities.

Scenario 9

A rugby coach decides to hold an open evening to encourage more young people from ethnic minorities to join his club. He sets a date and produces the following flyer to advertise the event:

He distributes the flyer to local shops and the PE department at the local comprehensive school, and leaves some at the club's reception.

Stop and consider

Do you think the rugby coach would attract many young people from ethnic minorities to the open evening? Why?

Come and have a go at rugby – join our scrum!

When?
Monday 5 March 2001

Where?
Anytown Rugby Club

Time?
7:00–9:00pm

Scenario 10

A coach runs junior sessions at a hockey club. Most of the girls who attend the sessions come from outside the local area and, although the coach doesn't have a problem with this, she also wants to encourage more local girls, most of whom are from ethnic minorities, to take part. She contacts local community leaders for advice on how to do this. They provide her with the information she needs and give their seal of approval to her plans.

The coach produces a promotional flyer to advertise the hockey sessions and circulates it round the local community via local schools, community centres, racial equality councils and community groups. The flyer contains:

- background information about the club

- details of the days and times at which junior sessions are held

- details of the cost of coaching sessions and concessionary rates made available by the local authority leisure department

- a message of support from the local community leaders.

The coach invites girls and their parents/carers to come and watch one of the sessions and meet the other female coaches who help to run them. She emphasises that it isn't necessary to wear any particular kind of clothing or shoes to take part in the coaching sessions, as long as they are comfortable, suitable and safe.

Stop and consider

Do you think the coach would attract many girls from ethnic minorities to her hockey sessions? Why?

As you read through the feedback below, try to relate it to your own situation and think about how you could make your coaching sessions more accessible to people from ethnic minorities.

Scenario 9

The rugby coach would have been unlikely to attract many young people from ethnic minorities to his open evening for the following reasons:

- He didn't liaise or consult with anyone from the local ethnic minority community about:
  - where the open evening was held
  - whether the date was suitable
  - whether the time was suitable
  - any other requirements people may have
  - the best way to promote the open evening.

If he had, he would have found out that:
  - young people would have been more likely to go to the open evening if it had been held at the local community centre, rather than the usual club venue
  - the date clashed with Eid ul-Fitr, an important Muslim festival that would prevent some potential participants from attending the open evening
  - the communal changing facilities at the club would put people off
  - local community leaders could have advertised the open evening on his behalf – the fact that they were supporting the event would have shown potential participants and their parents/carers that the club was serious about encouraging them to attend.

- He didn't explain that potential participants wouldn't need to wear special sports kit, or that all necessary equipment would be provided.
- He didn't provide any information about the coaches that would be running the open evening (ie whether there would be both male and female coaches present).
- He didn't include the cost (if any) of the open evening in his advert.
- The advert included a photo of a white rugby player – using a photo of players from ethnic minorities instead might have encouraged more people to attend the open evening.
- The open evening wasn't very well advertised.

Scenario 10

The coach would have been likely to succeed in making her hockey club accessible to all girls in the local area, regardless of ethnic origin, for the following reasons:

- She recognised that, although the majority of the girls in the local area are from ethnic minorities, very few attend her hockey sessions.
- Rather than assume that this was because they simply aren't interested in hockey, she realised that many of them might either be unaware that the hockey club existed, or would find it too daunting to join.
- She contacted local community leaders for advice on how to encourage girls from ethnic minorities to attend her club, and got their seal of approval for her plan.
- She advertised the hockey sessions in places that local girls regularly go to.
- She recognised the barriers that might prevent girls from ethnic minorities attending the sessions and made sure that the promotional flyer provided adequate reassurance:
  - She realised that they might have never heard of the club, so she provided a bit of background information, together with the days and times of the junior sessions.
  - She kept the cost of the coaching sessions to a minimum and agreed concessionary rates with the local authority for people on low incomes.

– She realised that parents/carers might be worried about allowing their daughters to attend the sessions, so she invited them to come along with their daughters to watch a session and meet the coaches.

– She realised that, due to religious or cultural reasons, it might not be appropriate for girls from ethnic minorities to attend coaching sessions run by male coaches, so she ensured that the sessions were run by female coaches.

– Similarly, she realised that, due to religious or cultural reasons, girls from ethnic minorities might not be able to wear certain kinds of clothing, so she emphasised that they could wear whatever they liked, providing it was comfortable, suitable and safe.

Points of interest

The coach in Scenario 10 took positive steps to provide sporting opportunities for girls from ethnic minorities. The contrast with Scenario 9 should help you appreciate just how important it is to be equitable in your coaching practice.

2.3 Women and Girls

The following panel identifies the key issues that may act as barriers to women and girls participating in sport.

BARRIERS TO PARTICIPATION IN SPORT

Practical Barriers
• Lack of time and childcare.
• Lack of money.
• Lack of transport.
• Personal safety.
• Funding.
• Access to facilities.
• Lack of female coaches.

Personal Barriers
• Body image.
• Clothing and equipment.
• Lack of self-confidence.
• Parental and adult influence.
• Peer group pressure.

Social and Cultural Barriers
• Male-dominated culture of sport.
• Indifference or negative attitude of some sporting organisations.
• Attitudes about sexuality.
• Attitudes about disability.
• Attitudes about ethnicity.
• Sexual harassment.
• Lack of role models, poor media coverage and provision of positive images of women and girls.

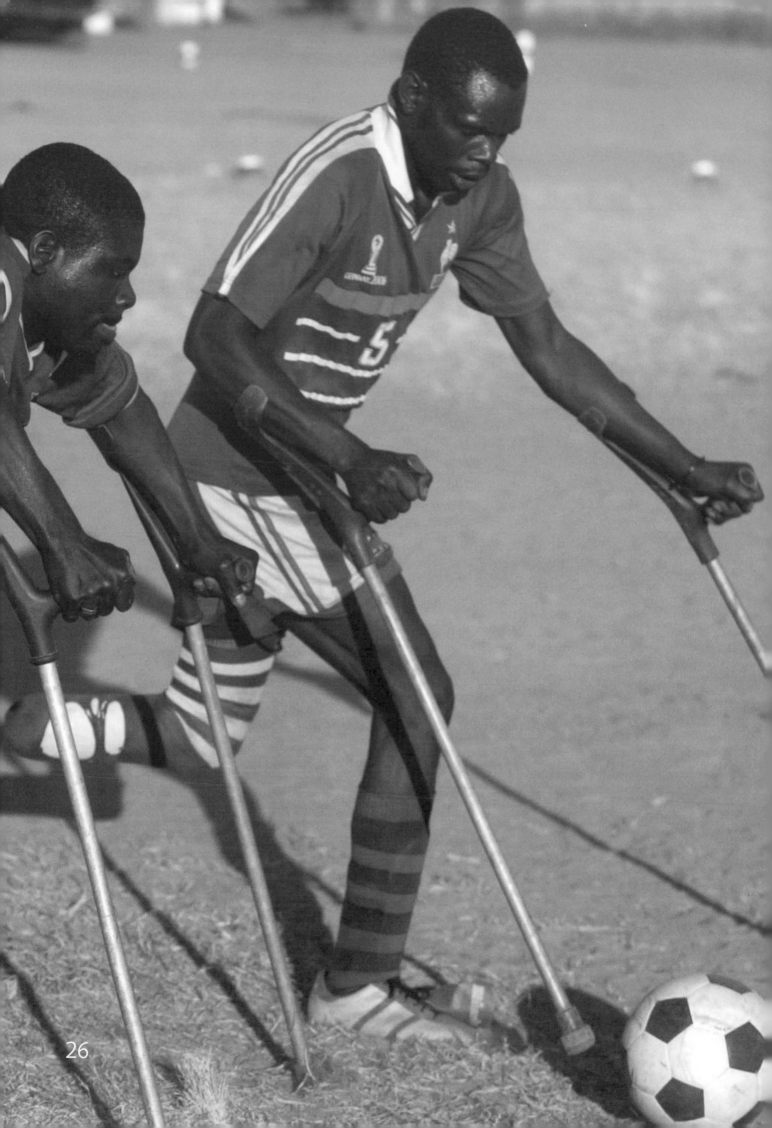

The following scenarios describe two different coaching situations. As you read through them, try to identify whether the coaches could have done more to make their coaching sessions more accessible to women and girls.

Scenario 11

Shiretown Leisure Centre is situated in the middle of a large industrial town. The centre was built about 20 years ago and has had the same manager all this time. He will be retiring in the next year or so and makes no secret of the fact that he can't wait to leave.

The centre is showing signs of wear and tear as the local authority have not had much money available to spend on it in recent years. A new leisure centre has been built at the edge of the town. It is modern and clean, with all the latest equipment and facilities, and a new, enthusiastic manager. The more forward-looking staff from the old centre have already got jobs at the new leisure centre, leaving the old centre short-staffed.

Tom is a self-employed football coach and is keen to encourage more women to play football. He decides to book the sports hall at the old leisure centre on Sunday evenings to run women's football sessions. He chooses the old leisure centre over the new one because it is cheaper and nearer to where he lives. He decides to run the sessions from 8:00–9:00pm as he is free at that time each week.

Tom designs a poster to advertise the football sessions:

Stop and consider

Do you think Tom would attract many women to his football sessions? Why?

GIRLS!
BEAT THE BOYS AT THEIR OWN GAME!

Women's Football Sessions

Where?
Shiretown Leisure Centre

When?
Every Sunday

Time?
8:00–9:00pm

Go on! Come and play a man's game!

© www.actionplus.co.uk

Scenario 12

A cricket coach is specifically responsible for drawing up training programmes for all new members at her club. She always meets new members individually and tries to make sure that the training programmes she subsequently comes up with complement their lifestyle and other commitments. She also provides them with a list of essential equipment they will need and explains that, if they like, a more experienced cricketer will be assigned to them to provide guidance and support.

While her general approach is the same for both male and female athletes, she recognises that there are specific things to bear in mind when preparing training programmes for female participants. The kinds of questions she asks new female members include:

- How many hours a week can you realistically devote to your training?
- When are the best times for you to train?
- How will you get to the club (eg own car, get a lift, public transport)?
- Training sessions may take place at other venues – would this be a problem?
- Would you prefer to attend mixed or women-only training sessions?
- Would you prefer to attend training sessions run by a male or female coach?
- Would you be interested in using the club crèche?
- Do you have any other requirements?

Stop and consider

Do you think the cricket coach would succeed in making her club accessible to women? Why?

As you read through the feedback below, try to relate it to your own situation and think about how you could make your coaching sessions more accessible to women and girls.

Scenario 11

Tom would have been unlikely to attract many women to his football sessions for the following reasons:

- Not many women were aware of the football sessions because they were only advertised at the leisure centre, which many had never been to before.
- The poster implied that football is a male preserve.
- Tom assumed that all women would jump at the chance of being able to play football when, in actual fact, they were more interested in other sports.
- The poster was offensive – this reflected badly on Tom both as a man and a coach, and several women decided that, although they quite fancied having a go at football, they didn't want to be coached by him.
- The poster didn't mention how much the sessions cost or whether equipment would be provided.
- The time of the session wasn't particularly convenient for most women.
- Many women didn't like being in the centre of town at that time of night.
- Public transport was practically non-existent on Sunday evenings.

- The leisure centre doesn't have a very welcoming environment:
  - The changing rooms aren't very clean.
  - The car park is badly lit at night.
  - The leisure-centre manager isn't particularly welcoming or enthusiastic.
  - The leisure-centre staff are overworked and take this out on the customers.
  - There are no childcare facilities.

Scenario 12

The cricket coach would have been likely to succeed in making her club accessible to women for the following reasons:

- She treated all new male and female club members equally. Women might be particularly reassured by the fact that they didn't need to fork out for lots of new equipment straight away and that they had the opportunity to receive guidance from a more experienced cricketer.
- In addition, she realised that there are special issues to consider when devising training programmes for women and, therefore, found out as much as she could about their requirements beforehand. This included finding out:
  - how much time women could devote to training and what the best times to train were – they often have other work and domestic commitments that have to take priority, so it is important that training times are convenient
  - how they would get to the club and making them aware that training sessions might be held at different venues, as it is important that all venues are convenient and safe to get to
  - whether they would prefer to attend mixed or women-only training sessions led by male or female coaches, as some women might feel more comfortable at women-only sessions run by a female coach
  - whether it would help if a crèche was available at the time of the training sessions, as this might be an important factor that influences women to continue their membership of the club
  - whether they had any other requirements, as it is important that the training programme caters for these.

Points of interest
The coach in Scenario 12 took positive steps to provide sporting opportunities for women. The contrast with Scenario 11 should help you to appreciate just how important it is to be equitable in your coaching practice.

2.4 People of Different Ages

The following panel identifies the key issues that may act as barriers to people of different ages participating in sport.

BARRIERS TO PARTICIPATION IN SPORT

Attitudes of Others
• Preconceptions about what people of different ages can achieve or do.

• Peer-group pressure.

• Lack of older or younger people being involved as participants or administrators.

Inconvenient Venue
• Lack of transport.

• Fear for personal safety getting to and from the venue.

Other Commitments
• School commitments have to take priority.

• Family commitments for older people.

• Too many conflicting interests.

Low Self-esteem
• Lack of confidence.

• Low expectations.

• Never done different sports before.

• No friends to take part with.

Poor Communication
• People of different ages not contacted.

• Poor media coverage of older people doing sport.

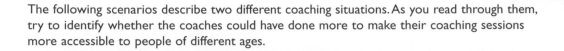

The following scenarios describe two different coaching situations. As you read through them, try to identify whether the coaches could have done more to make their coaching sessions more accessible to people of different ages.

Scenario 13

A tennis club has a large membership of all ages, which includes both males and females. The club publishes its annual tournament programme and has age groups up to 30 years of age, before grouping all those over 30 years together in one group. The competition committee decides that, as the future of the club is with the juniors, it will group the older ages together with both men and women in the same group, so as to give more time to all the junior tournaments. The committee decides that the over-30s tournament should only be played over one set – again, to leave more time for the three-set junior tournaments.

The junior tournaments are very successful and take up most of the day, and the club attracts new members in the junior section. The winners of the over-30s competitions are male and in their early 30s, having easily beaten the rest of the group.

Players over the age of 45 are told that their role is to support the tournaments by being umpires and line judges.

Stop and consider

Do you think this will encourage more people over the age of 30 to join the club? Why?

Scenario 14

A rugby club has an active mini-rugby section on a Sunday morning, but is short of volunteers, as three parents do all the kit washing, setting out of the pitch and organising of equipment, such as balls and other training aids.

The volunteer coordinator identifies specific roles for each person within the mini-rugby section in helping to set out the pitch, and encourages two young people to take photographs and arrange for permissions to be gained and articles to go in the local press.

The volunteer coordinator arranges informal coach/team manager sessions for parents/carers, as well as arranging an over-50s tag-rugby competition at the end of each Sunday session.

The three parents have a team of helpers and feel they are being supported by people of different ages.

Stop and consider

Do you think the club will increase the number of volunteers of different ages? Why?

As you read through the feedback below, try to relate it to your own situation and think about how you could make your coaching sessions more accessible to people of different ages.

Scenario 13

The club is unlikely to attract more people of an older age for the following reasons:

• It assumed that everyone over the age of 30 is at the same level of fitness and ability.

• It assumed that members over the age of 30 did not want to have any challenging competition.

• The organiser assumed that people were only interested in junior competitions.

• The organising committee didn't consult with members over the age of 30 about the tournament.

• The committee assumed that young people could not umpire and be line judges, and that this was an older person's role.

• The committee assumed that the longer game was suited to young people, and the older group could not cope with more than one set.

• The committee did not give equal time to all age groups to enable a suitable conclusion.

Scenario 14

The club is likely to succeed and increase the number of volunteers from different age ranges for the following reasons:

• It took positive action to encourage young people to take key volunteer roles.

• It provided a modified game to make the sport attractive to people of different ages.

• It involved all ages in the development of new activities which, in turn, will promote a greater loyalty to the club and its activities.

> **Points of interest**
> The coach in Scenario 14 took positive steps to provide sporting opportunities for people of different ages. The contrast with Scenario 13 should help you to appreciate just how important it is to be equitable in your coaching practice.

2.5 Economically Disadvantaged People

The following panel identifies the key issues that may act as barriers to people from economically disadvantaged backgrounds participating in sport.

BARRIERS TO PARTICIPATION IN SPORT

Attitudes of Others

• Preconceptions about the challenges that people with economic disadvantages face.

• Lack of understanding.

• Peer-group pressure.

Inconvenient Venue

• Lack of affordable transport.

• Cost of the venue.

• Safety travelling to and from the venue.

Low Self-esteem

• Lack of confidence.

• Low expectations.

• No friends to take part with.

The following scenarios describe two different coaching situations. As you read through them, try to identify whether the coaches could have done more to make their coaching sessions more accessible to economically disadvantaged people.

Scenario 15

James is a community volleyball coach and has decided to enter an under-16 team in the local league, playing home and away in the region. The team of under-16s is selected from two inner-city schools at which James has coached. He arranges a minibus and for the players to meet in the city centre ahead of away games. He also arranges two sessions of two hours each week; one for games and one for training at the local leisure centre, which is on a train route, with a train due every half-hour. The local leisure centre is not, however, on a bus route. The centre charges junior rates of £40 for the session, as the players are under 16 years of age.

James tells the players they must cover the cost of the court hire for both sessions, as, when they have a game, the away team doesn't pay for any court hire or officials. For the 10 players, this amounts to £4 per session. For away games, the local authority will pay petrol for the minibus and the players will be dropped off after the evening games in the city centre.

Stop and consider

Do you think James will be able to maintain the team throughout the season? Why?

Scenario 16

A group of schools play in the local schools' basketball league and most of the teams want to keep playing when they have finished school at 16 years of age. The local basketball club arranges an open session and invites all the players free of charge.

The club groups the players into six teams of mixed ability and from different schools; each team has a coach from the club. Every player is given a fixture list for the next 10 weeks for a league at one of the schools most central to the players. The games are modified to be completed in 40 minutes, thus allowing every team to play each week. To cover the costs, the players are charged £1 each to cover using the hall and to pay for kit and equipment. The local sports college director assists with paying for equipment and balls, and the regional development manager for basketball arranges basic refereeing for the older players, so they can referee other games in the league.

Stop and consider

Do you think the league will sustain itself? Why?

As you read through the feedback below, try to relate it to your own situation and think about how you could make your coaching sessions more accessible to people from disadvantaged backgrounds.

Scenario 15

The team is unlikely to succeed for the following reasons:

• It is too costly for the players to maintain this level of financial commitment.
• The coach is on his own and is likely to find it difficult to make sure players are able to keep going though the season.
• The leisure centre is a very expensive option for playing indoor team sports – a partnership with one of the schools may be a better option.
• The coach assumes that the players, although committed to the sport, will be able to find the money.
• The coach assumes that the players felt safe to meet and be dropped off in the city centre.

Scenario 16

The club is likely to succeed and increase the number of young people participating in it for the following reasons:

• It minimised the cost to participants.
• It took a positive step to minimise transport costs.
• It arranged the sessions at a venue that the players would know and feel comfortable with.
• It took positive action to encourage young people to take key volunteer roles.
• It provided a modified game to make the sport affordable.

The club in Scenario 16 took positive steps to provide sporting opportunities for people from disadvantaged backgrounds. The contrast with Scenario 15 should help you to appreciate just how important it is to be equitable and consider the personal circumstances of coaching practice.

2.6 Lesbian, Gay, Bisexual and Transgender People

The following panel identifies the key issues that may act as barriers to lesbian, gay, bisexual and transgender people participating in sport.

BARRIERS TO PARTICIPATION IN SPORT

Attitudes of Others
- Preconceptions about the challenges that lesbian, gay, bisexual and transgender people face.
- Lack of understanding.
- Ignorance about the meaning of 'sexuality'.
- Assumptions and attitudes.
- Peer-group pressure.
- The media's stereotypical view of lesbian, gay, bisexual and transgender people.
- Heterosexual people's 'fear' of lesbian, gay, bisexual and transgender people.

Low Self-esteem
- Lack of confidence.
- Low expectations.
- Fear of discrimination.
- No friends to take part with.

© Alan Ecwards

The following scenarios describe two different coaching situations. As you read through them, try to identify whether the coaches could have done more to make their coaching sessions more accessible to lesbian, gay, bisexual and transgender people.

Scenario 17

Two multi-sports clubs, one for women and one for men, decide to amalgamate to save costs and share a ground. The clubs agree the new committee structure, with both men and women equally represented on the committee. It is agreed that each team at all levels should have two coaches. The club agrees to have joint junior coaching sessions on a Sunday morning.

The clubs are discussing the committee and coaching structure and one of the men's club representatives asks that only one lesbian coach be allowed in each team. He states the reason why, as they will not be allowed into the female changing room prior to and after a game, and that they should change in the female toilets, with the other coach supervising the team.

He also asks that the balance of women on each committee be a balance of heterosexual and lesbian women. When challenged by the women members, he also asks that lesbian coaches be supervised at all times, as this is a child protection issue.

Stop and consider

Do you think the clubs will succeed in their amalgamation? Why?

Scenario 18

A governing body of sport is seeking to promote a new competition to recruit new members to different clubs in a particular local area. The governing body advertises in the local newspapers, on local radio and also uses different forms of media, modifying its website for people with a sight impairment. It also contacts the local gay and lesbian support groups, which recommend various media outlets to promote the new competition. The governing body changes its equity policy to take into account the Employment Equality (Sexual Orientation) Regulations 2003, recognising the need not to discriminate against lesbian, gay, bisexual and transgender people.

The governing body has entered a team in the International Gay and Lesbian Games, drawn from different teams across the country. This is promoted in the governing body magazine and the results celebrated on the website.

Stop and consider

Do you think the governing body will increase the number of lesbian, gay, bisexual and transgender people taking part in the sport? Why?

Scenario 17

The clubs are unlikely to succeed in their amalgamation for the following reasons:

• The men's committee discriminated against the women's selection.

• The men's committee made assumptions about the women's membership.

• The men's committee had responded to peer pressure.

Scenario 18

The governing body is likely to succeed and increase the number of young people participating in local clubs for the following reasons:

• It actively promoted a positive image of lesbian, gay, bisexual and transgender people.

• It had no preconceptions about anybody.

• It allocated resources to support specific entry into competition.

Points of interest

The governing body in Scenario 18 took positive steps to provide sporting opportunities for lesbian, gay, bisexual and transgender people. The contrast with Scenario 17 should help you to appreciate just how important it is to be equitable and consider the personal circumstances of coaching practice.

2.7 Summary

Although certain barriers to participation apply only to a specific target group, you will have noticed that many are common to all the key target groups. The diagram on the next page should help you to remember what these are.

The coaches in Scenarios 8 (page 19), 10 (page 23) 12 (page 28), 14 (page 31), 16 (page 34) and 18 (page 36) made every effort to be fair to everyone who wanted to be involved in their sport. This meant extra effort in some areas (eg arranging an additional judo club night) and relaxing rules in others (eg allowing girls at the netball club to wear whatever clothing they felt most comfortable in). In all six scenarios, this may have resulted in more people being involved in sport.

You should aim to put the same effort into your coaching practice. Don't worry if this seems a daunting prospect; the rest of this resource will help you to make your coaching sessions more accessible to the key target groups. Section Three starts by looking at the appropriate language and terminology to use when talking or referring to the key target groups.

SPORT

COACH

ASSUMPTIONS

- Which sports people are interested in
- Which sports people are able to do
- People's reasons for taking part in sport.

LACK OF KNOWLEDGE

- Indifference/negative attitudes
- Lack of encouragement
- Lack of understanding of needs and aspirations
- Lack of skills.

POOR COMMUNICATION

- Lack of communication with key target groups and organisations that can help
- Inappropriate language
- Inappropriate and inadequate marketing
- Lack of positive role models.

FACILITIES

INCONVENIENCE	LACK OF TRANSPORT	SAFETY FEARS	INADEQUATE FACILITIES AND EQUIPMENT

COST

SESSION FEE	KIT AND EQUIPMENT

TIME

INCONVENIENCE	OTHER COMMITMENTS
	• Work • Domestic • Other interests

PERSONAL ISSUES

LOW SELF-ESTEEM	FEAR OF DISCRIMINATION AND UNWELCOMING ENVIRONMENT	CULTURAL/ RELIGIOUS INFLUENCES

PARTICIPATION

Section 3

Language and Terminology

3.0 What's In It For You?

In any coaching situation, it is important to treat your participants fairly and with respect – language has a vital role to play in this. In order to create a positive, welcoming coaching environment, it is essential that the language you use is:

• sensitive

• appropriate

• relevant

• consistent.

Language is continually evolving as awareness and attitudes change. For example, several words used in the context of disability, which were acceptable in the past, are now no longer used. *Spastic* used to be a common term, but has now been replaced by *person with cerebral palsy*. This was mainly due to the misuse of the term, which subsequently became one of ridicule.

By the end of this section, you should be:

• aware of the appropriate terminology to use when referring to people from each of the key target groups, both during and outside your coaching sessions

• able to identify examples of acceptable and unacceptable terminology.

The information in this section is by no means exhaustive, nor a definitive guide – the terms included here may be revised or disappear in the future and other terms may appear.

3.1 Disabled People

The following table contains some of the common terms associated with disability. The left-hand column lists terms used in the past, which should now be avoided; the right-hand column lists more acceptable alternatives. Some of the terms are also mentioned in Appendix D.

Unacceptable	Acceptable
the blind	blind and partially sighted people/ visually impaired people
the deaf/hard of hearing/ profoundly deaf	deaf or hard-of-hearing people/ people with a hearing impairment
deaf and dumb	deaf without speech
the disabled/the handicapped/ cripples/invalids	disabled people
disabled toilets	accessible toilets
dumb/mute	person with a speech impairment/ speech-impaired person
an epileptic	person with epilepsy
handicap	disability/impairment
mentally disabled/subnormal/ abnormal/retarded/backward	person with learning disabilities
Mongolism	Down's syndrome
normal people/able-bodied people	non-disabled people
patient	person
spastic	person with cerebral palsy
special needs	(additional) needs
wheelchair bound/ confined to a wheelchair	wheelchair user
wheelchair coach	coach
victim of/stricken by/crippled by/ afflicted by/sufferer of	has/with (the particular condition)

3.2 People from Ethnic Minorities

As with terms relating to disability, many of those associated with people from ethnic minorities should be avoided, even if they were regarded as acceptable in the past. Examples include:

Term	Reasons to Avoid
Chink	Used to refer to people of perceived Chinese descent. Describes their eye slits or chinks. Considered extremely derogatory[1].
Coconut	Term used to denounce another who is of black or brown heritage, but not reflecting the perceived values of the black or brown community (ie 'black on the outside, white on the inside')[1].
Coloured	Regarded as outdated and generally offensive to many black people. When applied to South Africa, the term reflects issues of ethnic divide and apartheid[2].
Half-caste	Regarded as outdated and racist. Implies 'half a person'[2].
Nigger	An offensive and derogatory term used by white people towards black people during the slave trade in the southern states of the USA. Sometimes used now in black rap songs, as a term between one black person and another. Use of the word is often perceived as extremely offensive if used by a white person in any context[1].
Non-white	Implies that *white* is the generic term for all people[2].
Paki	An offensive and derogatory term often used to refer to people from Pakistan, or Asian people in general[2].

[1] Adapted from Google Dictionary.

[2] Taken from the British Sociological Association website (www.britsoc.co.uk).

You should always use acceptable terminology when referring to people from ethnic minorities. The most common terms you need to be aware of include:

Term	Guidance
Asian people	Use this term when referring to people from the Indian subcontinent – India, Pakistan, Bangladesh and Kashmir. Bear in mind that some people may prefer to refer to their country of origin (eg Bangladeshi, Indian, Pakistani) rather than to the general term Asian, which includes a wide variety of different cultural and ethnic groups. Other people may prefer to be referred to neither as Asian nor by their country of origin if several generations of their family have been living in Britain[1].
Black people	Use this term when referring to people of African, Caribbean and South Asian origin. However, remember that some Asian groups in Britain object to being referred to as *black*; some people believe the term confuses a number of ethnic groups, which should be treated separately. One solution to this is to refer to black **peoples** or black **communities** in the plural to imply that there is a variety of such groups. You should also be aware that *black* can also be used in a racist sense in certain contexts[2].
People from ethnic minorities	Use this term when referring collectively to people of different ethnic origins and backgrounds.

A more detailed list of terminology associated with people from ethnic minorities is provided in Appendix E.

[1] and [2] Based on information provided on the British Sociological Association website (www.britsoc.co.uk).

3.3 Women and Girls

Although often unintentional, many people refer or talk to women and girls using terms which are sometimes perceived as patronising and offensive. The table below shows which terms to avoid, together with more acceptable alternatives.

Context	Avoid	Use
Referring/talking to a group of female participants	Birds/chicks/ girls/ladies	Everyone/everybody/ women/females
Referring/talking to an individual female participant	Bird/chick/dear/ duck/love/pet	Name the participant wants to be known by/woman/female

Note: Not everyone will find the terms in the Avoid column patronising and offensive — some people may be quite happy for you to use them. Use your discretion when talking or referring to women and girls in your coaching sessions — if in doubt, ask participants how they would prefer to be addressed.

3.4 People of Different Ages

Although often used in jest or as a compliment, the identification of age can sometimes demonstrate a perception that a particular group or individual cannot carry out a particular activity.

People over the age of 20 are likely to live more than 20 years longer than their parents, due to advances in medical treatment, diet and lifestyle. Therefore, decisions should be made on the basis of ability rather than age. The same goes for young people, as well as mature people, and the expectations of younger people should not be prejudiced by assumptions about a particular age group.

3.5 Economically Disadvantaged People

The identification of people who are regarded as economically disadvantaged is very difficult, as many people from other groups can also fall into this category. Many factors may lead to a person being economically disadvantaged. These include:

• where they live (both urban and rural)

• health problems

• their status as refugees and asylum seekers

• those at risk of offending, offenders and ex-offenders

• whether or not they are old

• whether or not they have a disability

• if they are young people at risk

• if they are living in poverty

• if they are unemployed.

3.6 Lesbian, Gay, Bisexual and Transgender People

Sometimes, people who object to lesbian, gay, bisexual or transgender people are called homophobic. Homophobia is a fear of and/or hostility towards gay people or homosexuality. Homophobia is often expressed visibly, audibly and sometimes violently. Research carried out in 1996 by gay-rights group Stonewall showed that gay people had experienced more extreme homophobia as young people than as adults. The research found that, as young people, 90% of the respondents had been called names and nearly 50% had been violently attacked. In areas of England, homophobic bullying in schools has now reached the point where young people being bullied have special homework clubs.

As with terms relating to disability and ethnicity, many of those associated with lesbian, gay, bisexual and transgender people should be avoided, even if they were regarded as acceptable in the past. Examples include:

Term	Reasons to Avoid
Queer	A term used to describe a gay man, implying he is not right. A very derogatory term.
Straight	Implying that someone is not gay, lesbian, bisexual or transgender, and that anyone who is not heterosexual is not as good as a heterosexual.
Bent	A derogative comment towards someone who is gay, lesbian, bisexual or of transgender.
Homo	A derogatory term for someone who is gay or lesbian.

3.7 Summary

You should now be familiar with which terms to use and which to avoid when talking or referring to people from the key target groups. The next activity asks you to identify examples of acceptable and unacceptable terminology.

ACTIVITY 2

The table below contains a number of statements about people from the key target groups. Decide whether each statement is acceptable and write **Yes** or **No** in the second column. If a statement is not acceptable, write a more acceptable alternative in the third column.

	Statement	Acceptable?	More Acceptable Alternative (if appropriate)
1	Harpal runs coaching sessions for both able-bodied and disabled gymnasts.		
2	Tony is a swimming coach, aiming to encourage more non-white people in the local area to take up swimming.		
3	Sophie contacts her governing body to find out more about coaching participants suffering from Down's syndrome.		
4	Matthew makes sure his coaching venue has accessible toilets for wheelchair users.		
5	Daniel is asked to coach a women's rugby team. He declines, saying he 'doesn't think rugby is a birds' game'.		
6	Nawal is asked to start coaching a group of mentally disabled teenagers who are interested in taking up badminton.		

Statement	Acceptable?	More Acceptable Alternative (if appropriate)
7 Hassiba runs basketball coaching sessions at her local community centre specifically aimed at women and girls from black and Asian communities.		
8 Desmond contacts British Blind Sport for information on modifying sports for visually impaired people.		
9 Carla is a wheelchair tennis coach.		
10 'OK, Sandra – can you return to your half of the court and prepare to serve again?' asked the squash coach.		

Feedback

Statement	Acceptable?	More Acceptable Alternative (if appropriate)
1 Harpal runs coaching sessions for both able-bodied and disabled gymnasts.	NO	• Harpal runs coaching sessions for both **non-disabled** and disabled gymnasts. • Harpal runs coaching sessions for **gymnasts of all abilities**.
2 Tony is a swimming coach, aiming to encourage more non-white people in the local area to take up swimming.	NO	• Tony is a swimming coach, aiming to encourage more **people from local ethnic minority communities** to take up swimming.
3 Sophie contacts her governing body to find out more about coaching participants suffering from Down's syndrome.	NO	• Sophie contacts her governing body to find out more about coaching participants **who have/with** Down's syndrome.
4 Matthew makes sure his coaching venue has accessible toilets for wheelchair users.	YES	• It is appropriate to refer to **accessible toilets** and **wheelchair users**.
5 Daniel is asked to coach a women's rugby team. He declines, saying he 'doesn't think rugby is a birds' game'.	NO	• Not only is Daniel wrong to refer to women as 'birds', but he is also wrong to suggest that women cannot and should not play rugby!
6 Nawal is asked to start coaching a group of mentally disabled teenagers who are interested in taking up badminton.	NO	• Nawal is asked to start coaching a group of teenagers **with learning disabilities**.
7 Hassiba runs basketball coaching sessions at her local community centre specifically aimed at women and girls from black and Asian communities.	YES	• It is appropriate to refer to **black and Asian communities**.

Statement	Acceptable	More Acceptable Alternative (if appropriate)
8 Desmond contacts British Blind Sport for information on modifying sports for visually impaired people.	YES	• It is appropriate to refer to **visually impaired people**.
9 Carla is a wheelchair tennis coach.	NO	• Carla is a **tennis** coach.
10 'OK, Sandra – can you return to your half of the court and prepare to serve again?' asked the squash coach.	YES	• It is appropriate to address any participant by the name by which they wish to be known.

Remember!

- Use language that is sensitive, appropriate and relevant.

- Conversation between friends is different to conversation with people you don't know well.

- If you are unsure which terms are acceptable or unacceptable, ask the people you are coaching.

- Everybody has the right to choose how they wish to be referred to – not everyone may choose to be referred to in the same way.

- If people refer to themselves in a way you find offensive, you don't have to use that word just because they do.

© Alan Edwards

Using appropriate language and terminology is just one way of ensuring your coaching sessions are as equitable as possible. Section Four looks at ways of applying and extending your existing coaching skills and experience to meet the needs of your participants.

Section 4

Tips for More Equitable Coaching

4.0 What's In It For You?

You may find the prospect of coaching different people in your sport a bit daunting, particularly if you don't have much previous experience. But it's not a case of having to learn a whole new set of coaching skills, it's more about *applying* and *extending* your existing skills and experience to meet the needs of your participants. *Applying your existing skills* means treating the key target groups the same as you would any other participants – that is:

• communicating effectively to people in a way they feel comfortable with

• planning coaching sessions and programmes to meet the needs of participants

• analysing and evaluating performance

• creating a safe environment

• being open-minded in developing your coaching skills and knowledge.

Extending your skills means understanding the additional issues you need to consider when coaching disabled people, people from ethnic minorities, women and girls, people from disadvantaged backgrounds, people of different sexuality and of different ages.

By the end of this section, you should be:

• aware of the specific issues you need to consider when coaching the key target groups

• able to identify ways in which coaches make their sessions accessible and appropriate for the key target groups in specific coaching scenarios.

4.1 Disabled People

DON'T MAKE ASSUMPTIONS

- Don't assume that, just because not many disabled people currently attend your coaching sessions, they simply aren't interested in your sport. Think back to the barriers to participation identified in Section 2.1.

- Don't assume that disabled people just take part in sport because it's therapeutic. They participate in sport for the same reasons as non-disabled people (eg to improve fitness, make friends, as a personal challenge, for competition). The benefits of sport are also the same (eg improving confidence and self-esteem, handling pressure and stress).

- Don't make too many assumptions about whether people can take part in your sport – you'll be surprised how easily most sports can be adapted and how many disabled people can be successful with appropriate support from their coach.

- Coaching disabled people doesn't necessarily mean providing separate coaching sessions – it is often possible to integrate disabled people into existing sessions.

Appendix F provides a useful summary of the different levels of integration possible. The level selected will depend on:

- the type of sport
- the views of the disabled person
- your views
- the views of other participants
- the views of others (eg parents, helpers).

ACT APPROPRIATELY

- In order to create a positive, welcoming coaching environment, make sure you use language that is sensitive, appropriate and relevant, so as not to upset or offend disabled people. It can be difficult to know what is acceptable and unacceptable – refer back to Section Three for guidance.

COMMUNICATE

- Consulting your participants about their needs and aspirations is important, regardless of their ability. So, as well as finding out about the broader issues associated with coaching disabled people, it's also important to consult disabled people individually about:

    - their specific needs
    - what kind of support they will need from you
    - what kind of specialist equipment they will need
    - their existing skills and fitness levels
    - what they hope to achieve from the coaching sessions
    - other issues (eg transport, costs).

- Use language that is sensitive, appropriate and relevant both during and outside your coaching sessions (see Section 3.1 for more information).

- Effective communication is a key element of successful coaching. You may find there are additional challenges to the way you communicate when coaching disabled people. It is important that you establish the best way to communicate with individuals.

Appendix D provides some useful suggestions on how to communicate effectively with disabled people.

- Advertise your coaching sessions adequately, appropriately and in the right places (eg schools attended by disabled people). Include positive images of disabled people in any promotional material you produce. If required, provide promotional material in alternative formats (eg large print, audio).

- Encourage other coaches at your club to attend workshops/courses relating to disability issues:

    sports coach UK workshops:

    - Equity in Your Coaching
    - How to Coach Disabled People in Sport (Coaching Essentials Workshop)
    - Coaching Disabled Performers (Develop Your Coaching Workshop)

Workshop dates and locations are available from the Workshop Booking Centre.

See page 128 for contact details of the Workshop Booking Centre.

Governing body sport-specific courses

Many governing bodies of sport run courses designed to assist those coaching disabled performers. Find out what your governing body of sport has to offer.

CATER FOR DIFFERENT NEEDS

- It is important to be aware of your responsibilities when coaching disabled people – you owe them a greater duty of care[1] than you would to non-disabled people.

- It is important to balance the need for greater duty of care with the wishes and aspirations of the disabled people being coached. Some may need more support than others (eg a person with learning disabilities may not appreciate the dangers of walking across a javelin throwing area). It is therefore essential to strike a balance between appropriate support and maintaining the independence of individual participants.

- Become as familiar as possible with the needs of people with different impairments and the requirements of your sport – particularly about the rules and equipment for disabled people.

- Identify the relevant safety and medical implications of working with groups with specific impairment.

- Carry out a complete risk assessment of your coaching sessions and the venue(s) they will be held in.

- Find out about any specialist equipment that may be required to coach disabled people in your sport. The following organisations can provide information on equipment that exists and how to obtain it:

  – Disability Information Trust (www.justmobility.co.uk)

  – Disabled Living Foundation (www.dlf.org.uk)

  – Equal Adventure Developments (www.equaladventure.co.uk)

  – Remap (www.remap.org.uk).

- Make sure your coaching sessions are held at convenient venues with adequate facilities that cater for disabled people.

- Some disabled people may wish to compete. Find out about the opportunities available for competition at local, regional and national levels, so that you can advise and direct disabled people appropriately. You will also need to know about the classification systems that operate in disabled sport to ensure that competitions are fair and enjoyable.

SEEK ADVICE

If in doubt, contact organisations that can offer help and advice.

See pages 141–154 for contact details.

Bear the information in the panels in mind as you complete the next activity.

[1] See pages 107–108 for further information about duty of care.

ACTIVITY 3

Read through the following scenario. As you do, try to identify the ways in which Shaheed makes his coaching sessions accessible and appropriate for the deaf and hearing-impaired teenagers, and list them in the space provided at the end of the scenario.

Scenario 19

Shaheed is a qualified tennis coach. His local deaf club asks him if he would be willing to coach a group of deaf and hearing-impaired children who are keen to take up tennis – Shaheed agrees.

Because he has never coached disabled people before, Shaheed contacts the British Deaf Sports Council for advice. He also attends a couple of workshops to help him understand the requirements of coaching disabled people – the sports coach UK introductory workshop 'Coaching Disabled Performers' and the LTA Short Course 'Working with Disabilities'.

Once his coaching sessions get under way, Shaheed finds that being able to communicate appropriately with the participants is a vital part of successful coaching. He also finds that, by getting to know the participants well, he is able to adapt his existing coaching skills to suit their individual needs.

Stop and consider

How does Shaheed ensure his coaching sessions are accessible and appropriate for the deaf and hearing-impaired children? List the ways in the space provided below.

Now turn over.

Feedback

Shaheed makes his coaching sessions as equitable as possible by:

• gaining information about coaching deaf and hearing-impaired people (ie contacting the British Deaf Sports Council)

• attending appropriate coach education courses (ie sports coach UK and LTA workshops)

• communicating effectively and appropriately with his participants

• assessing the individual needs of his participants and adapting his existing coaching skills to meet them.

© www.actionplus.co.uk

4.2 People from Ethnic Minorities

▶ DON'T MAKE ASSUMPTIONS

- Don't assume that, just because not many people from ethnic minorities currently attend your coaching sessions, they simply aren't interested in your sport. Think back to the barriers to participation identified in Section 2.2.

- Remember, the reasons people participate in sport are the same, regardless of ethnic origin (eg to improve fitness, make friends, as a personal challenge, for competition). The benefits of sport are also the same (eg improving confidence and self-esteem, handling pressure and stress). Try to raise awareness of these benefits – if possible, use positive role models from ethnic minorities.

▶ COMMUNICATE

- Consult with relevant organisations and community leaders about issues such as:
  - appropriate venues, days and times for coaching sessions
  - specific requirements people from ethnic minorities may have
  - appropriate means of advertising your coaching sessions.

  Doing this will prove to people from ethnic minorities that you are serious about encouraging them to join your coaching sessions.

- Use language that is sensitive, appropriate and relevant both during and outside your coaching sessions (see Section 3.2 for more information).

- People from different ethnic backgrounds will have different needs and aspirations. It is, therefore, important to consult with individuals to find out about:
  - any specific requirements
  - what kind of support they will need from you
  - their existing skills and fitness levels
  - what they hope to achieve from the coaching sessions
  - other issues (eg transport, costs).

  If you are coaching children and young people from ethnic minorities, don't forget to consult with their parents/carers too, to gain their support.

- Advertise your coaching sessions adequately and appropriately – make sure any promotional material you produce includes information that is relevant to people from ethnic minorities (eg clothing and equipment required, whether male and female coaches are available). Include positive images of people from ethnic minorities in any promotional material you produce.

- Encourage other coaches at your club to attend the sports coach UK workshop 'Equity in Your Coaching'. Workshop dates and locations are available from the Workshop Booking Centre.

See page 128 for contact details of the Workshop Booking Centre.

CATER FOR DIFFERENT NEEDS

- Be aware of different religious/cultural requirements. For example:
  - It may not be appropriate for women and girls from ethnic minorities to attend coaching sessions run by male coaches, so you would need to ensure that sessions run by female coaches are available.
  - It may be necessary to relax any club rules on clothing worn during coaching sessions. People from ethnic minorities are often required to wear certain items of clothing for religious/cultural reasons (eg a turban). Similarly, they may be unable to wear certain kinds of clothing (eg a sports skirt). Reassure participants that they can wear whatever they like, providing the clothing worn is comfortable, suitable and safe.
  - It may not be appropriate for people to take part in sport during important religious festivals. Appendix C provides a brief summary of the main festivals celebrated by people from different religions. You should always take these into account when scheduling coaching sessions, events or competitions. The list in Appendix C is not exhaustive, so remember to consult with individual participants too.
  - Be aware of other issues relating to religious festivals that may affect performance (eg fasting).
- Hold your coaching sessions at convenient venues. Don't just expect people to come to your club – try to run sessions within their community environment. Make sure the venues have adequate facilities that cater for the needs of people from ethnic minorities (eg cubicles, rather than communal changing areas).
- Be prepared to adapt your coaching skills, if necessary.

ACT APPROPRIATELY

- In order to create a positive, welcoming coaching environment, make sure you use language that is sensitive, appropriate and relevant, so as not to upset or offend people from ethnic minorities. It can be difficult to know what is acceptable and unacceptable – refer back to Section Three for guidance.

SEEK ADVICE

If in doubt, contact organisations that can offer help and advice.

See pages 141–154 for contact details.

Bear the information in the panels in mind as you complete the activity on the next page.

ACTIVITY 4

Read through the following scenario. As you do, try to identify the ways in which Kath makes her coaching scheme accessible and appropriate for women and girls from ethnic minorities, and list them in the space provided on the next page.

Scenario 20

Kath is a coach at a local rowing club. She realises that very few women and girls from ethnic minorities are members of her club and wants to do something to encourage more to take up rowing.

She arranges to meet up with local community leaders to discuss her plan. In particular, she asks them about the barriers that might discourage women and girls from joining the club (eg cost, transport, time of coaching sessions, equipment required) and the best way to advertise the coaching scheme she intends to launch. The local community leaders think Kath's scheme is a great idea and say they will do everything they can to help her out. They put her in touch with a black female rower from the local area to feature as a positive role model in the promotional material Kath intends to produce.

Kath decides to run two sets of coaching sessions, one at the local community centre for those who would rather have a go at rowing on dry land before venturing onto the water and the other at a local lake for those who would rather go straight out onto the water. She enlists the help of other coaches from her rowing club, including two female coaches.

She produces a promotional flyer to advertise the coaching scheme, which includes the following information:

• Details of the two sets of coaching sessions on offer (ie one on dry land, the other on the water), with a note explaining that potential participants are free to swap to the other scheme after the introductory session if they wish.

• Details of the date, time and venue of the first sessions, with a note asking potential participants to let her know if these aren't convenient.

• Information about the cost of the coaching sessions – the first one will be free, subsequent ones will be heavily subsidised.

• Details of free transport available to and from the coaching venues.

• The names of the female coaches who will be helping Kath to run the two schemes.

• Reassurance that all necessary equipment will be provided – all potential participants need to bring is themselves!

• Reassurance that no special kit needs to be worn – as long as it's suitable and safe for rowing in, potential participants can wear whatever they feel most comfortable in.

• A message of encouragement from the local community leaders and local black female rower.

Kath distributes the promotional flyers via routes identified by the local community leaders (eg local community centres, inserted in local community free newspaper).

Stop and consider

How does Kath make her coaching scheme accessible and appropriate for women and girls from ethnic minorities? List the ways in the space provided below.

Feedback

Kath made her coaching sessions as equitable as possible by:

• identifying that very few women and girls from ethnic minorities were members of her rowing club and deciding to do something to encourage more to take up rowing

• meeting and consulting with local community leaders to find out how best to tailor her rowing schemes to meet the needs of women and girls from ethnic minorities

• using a positive role model

• using local facilities and providing free transport

• trying to anticipate the most appropriate dates and times to run the coaching sessions, but asking potential participants to get back to her if these are inconvenient

• providing free/subsidised coaching sessions

• enlisting the help of other female coaches from ethnic minorities

• providing all necessary equipment

• having a relaxed dress code

• ensuring the promotional flyer includes the kind of information women and girls from ethnic minorities will want to know

• publicising the support of local community leaders and the positive role model

• distributing the promotional flyers via appropriate routes.

© Alan Edwards

4.3 Women and Girls

DON'T MAKE ASSUMPTIONS

- Don't assume that, just because not many women and girls currently attend your coaching sessions, they simply aren't interested in your sport. Think back to the barriers to participation identified in Section 2.3.

- Don't assume that all women and girls are interested in the same kinds of activities – offer as wide a choice as possible and tailor your coaching programmes to meet their different needs.

- Don't make assumptions about the capabilities of women and girls in your sport. All participants, regardless of gender, should be assessed individually to establish their current level of ability.

COMMUNICATE

- Consult women and girls to find out what sort of activities they are interested in (eg interviews, questionnaires).

- Use language that is sensitive, appropriate and relevant both during and outside your coaching sessions (see Section 3.3 for more information).

- Do not refer to a woman's marital status.

- Include positive images of women and girls in any promotional material you produce. These should reflect real women and girls in society, not just the model-like perfection frequently portrayed in women's magazines.

- Encourage other coaches at your club to attend the sports coach UK workshop 'Equity in Your Coaching'. Workshop dates and locations are available from the Workshop Booking Centre.

See page 128 for contact details of the Workshop Booking Centre.

CATER FOR DIFFERENT NEEDS

- Understand the barriers that may discourage women and girls from participating in sport. For example:
  - Many women and girls don't feel comfortable or confident at mixed sessions (eg fear of ridicule or abuse, don't want to look silly, worried about their appearance).
  - Many women and girls underestimate their levels of competence in sport and may think they aren't experienced or good enough to join coaching sessions.
  - Personal safety is a particularly important issue for women and girls (eg transport, car-park lighting, access to venue, timing).
- Understand the legal requirements under which you practise. Under the terms of sex discrimination legislation, it is only acceptable to run women-only coaching sessions if:
  - female participants are likely to suffer serious embarrassment at the presence of male participants
  - female participants are likely to be in a state of undress and might reasonably object to the presence of male participants
  - physical contact is likely between participants of the opposite sex, and women and girls might reasonably object to this
  - coaching sessions are run by a single-sex voluntary group.

  In all cases, you need to be able to justify running women-only sessions (eg expressed preferences from existing or potential participants, religious/cultural reasons, results of research/surveys). You may also need to restrict the running of coaching sessions to female coaches and consider allowing female spectators only, or perhaps no spectators at all.

See page 95 for further information on the Sex Discrimination Act 1975, 1986 and 1999.

- Take time to find out what the 'player pathway' is for females in your sport. This may mirror that of male counterparts, but there are some differences. If you are to support participants to achieve their full potential, then you need to know where to direct them.
- Promote female athletes in your area as role models for girls at your club. Due to the relative lack of media coverage, there may be a perception that females can't aspire to high levels of performance in sport. Working with governing bodies of sport and CPS to address this issue through your club could help to change this perception.
- There is also a relative lack of female coaches. By becoming the best coach you can be and ensuring all those you coach gain a positive experience, you could become a role model yourself and inspire the next generation of female sports coaches.
- Once you have attracted female participants to your club, it is important that they feel welcome and part of the club. Wherever possible, engage them in the decision-making process. You can't do this on your own – work with other officers and members in the club to develop a positive and welcoming environment.
- Particularly for the younger participants, place the emphasis on the development of core skills in line with the LTAD model. Competition has its place, but females are more likely to continue participating if they feel comfortable in their own skin, as a lack of self-esteem often prevents them taking part. Focus on individual needs, allowing each individual to progress at their own level.
- Be aware of the physiological differences between male and female participants of different ages that may affect performance (eg children's development, conditions that specifically affect female participants, such as osteoporosis or menstruation).
- Ensure your coaching sessions are held at easily accessible venues which provide a welcoming environment for women and girls, both in terms of staff and facilities.

- Although it may be difficult to find a time to suit everyone, establish the most convenient times for women to attend your coaching sessions. Women often have the same work commitments as men, so don't automatically assume you can run women's sessions during weekday off-peak periods only.

- Consider providing free or subsidised transport to and from your coaching sessions – this will benefit women and girls who would otherwise have difficulty getting to the venue, as well as those who feel uncomfortable about travelling alone to coaching sessions.

- If your coaching venue doesn't already have one, consider providing a crèche for women bringing young children with them.

- Make sure your coaching sessions are reasonably priced, but remember that pricing policies must not discriminate between men and women. Female participants cannot be offered discounts that are not available to the same category of male participants.

- Consider alternatives to expensive equipment and kit (eg allowing a relaxed dress code).

ACT APPROPRIATELY

- In order to create a positive, welcoming coaching environment, make sure you use language that is sensitive, appropriate and relevant, so as not to upset or offend women and girls. It can be difficult to know what is acceptable and unacceptable – refer back to Section Three for guidance.

- During mixed coaching sessions:
  - use both male and female participants to demonstrate new skills
  - match participants by skill, rather than gender, when dividing them into pairs or small groups to learn new skills
  - check that participants feel comfortable about pair/group work with members of the opposite sex.

- As a general rule:
  - refrain from overfamiliarity and respect participants' individual space
  - never make comments or remarks of a sexual nature
  - if some coaching techniques require physical contact or support, check your governing body of sport guidelines and ask the participant's permission first. Touching can be okay and appropriate, as long as it is neither intrusive nor disturbing
  - avoid going into changing facilities, especially while participants are getting changed. If it cannot be avoided, always ask participants' permission first
  - avoid spending time alone with individual participants
  - avoid giving participants a lift to and from coaching sessions in your car, unless absolutely necessary, particularly if you are likely to be alone together.

SEEK ADVICE

If in doubt, contact organisations that can offer help and advice.

See pages 141–154 for contact details.

ACTIVITY 5

Read through the following scenario. As you do, try to identify the ways in which Jane makes her coaching sessions accessible and appropriate for both men and women, and list them in the space provided at the end of the scenario.

Scenario 21

Jane is a coach at a local cricket club. She decides to set up coaching sessions for beginners, which will be open to both men and women. She runs an introductory session to assess the existing skills of the participants. This includes drills and technique work in batting, bowling and fielding.

She starts off by observing the participants and later divides them up into pairs, matching similarly skilled players, having first made sure that the participants feel comfortable about working with members of the opposite sex.

When introducing new skills, Jane is as likely to ask a woman to demonstrate as she is to ask a man. She is sensitive in her use of language and uses both men and women as positive role models for particular coaching points.

Stop and consider

How does Jane make her coaching session accessible and appropriate for both male and female participants? List the ways in the space provided below.

Now turn over.

Feedback

Jane made her coaching session accessible and appropriate for both men and women by:

• observing the participants to assess individual skill levels and technique

• checking that all participants felt comfortable about working with members of the opposite sex

• pairing similarly skilled players

• asking both men and women to demonstrate when introducing new skills

• being sensitive in her use of language

• using both men and women as positive role models.

© Alan Edwards

4.4 People of Different Ages

DON'T MAKE ASSUMPTIONS

- Don't assume that, just because people are younger or older than the norm, they simply aren't interested in your sport. Think back to the barriers to participation identified in Section 2.4.

- Remember, the reasons people participate in sport are the same, regardless of age (eg for fun, to improve fitness, make friends, as a personal challenge, for competition). The benefits of sport are also the same (eg improving confidence and self-esteem, handling pressure and stress). Try to raise awareness of these benefits – if possible, use people of different ages as positive role models.

COMMUNICATE

- Consult with relevant organisations about issues such as:
  - appropriate venues, days and times for coaching sessions
  - specific requirements for people of different ages
  - appropriate means of advertising your coaching sessions.

  Doing this will prove to people of different ages that you are serious about encouraging them to join your coaching sessions.

- Use language that is sensitive, appropriate and relevant both during and outside your coaching sessions (see Section 3.4 for more information).

- People of different ages will have different needs and aspirations. It is, therefore, important to consult with individuals to find out about:
  - any specific requirements
  - what kind of support they will need from you
  - existing skills and fitness levels
  - what they hope to achieve from the coaching sessions
  - other issues (eg transport, costs).

  If you are coaching children and young people, don't forget to consult with their parents/carers too, to gain their support.

- Advertise your coaching sessions adequately and appropriately – make sure any promotional material you produce includes information that is relevant to people of different ages.

- Encourage other coaches at your club to attend the sports coach UK workshops 'Equity in Your Coaching' and 'Coaching Children and Young Performers'. Workshop dates and locations are available from the Workshop Booking Centre.

See page 128 for contact details of the Workshop Booking Centre.

ACT APPROPRIATELY

• In order to create a positive, welcoming coaching environment, make sure you use language that is sensitive, appropriate and relevant, so as not to upset or offend people of different ages. It can be difficult to know what is acceptable and unacceptable – refer back to Section Three for guidance.

SEEK ADVICE

If in doubt, contact organisations that can offer help and advice.

See pages 141–154 for contact details.

Bear the information in the panels in mind as you complete the activity on the next page.

© Alan Edwards

ACTIVITY 6

Read through the following scenario. As you do, try to identify the ways in which Peter makes his coaching sessions accessible and appropriate to people of different ages, and list them in the space provided at the end of the scenario.

Scenario 22

Peter is a multi-sports coach in a rural community and is having difficulty getting enough people in different age groups to reach a critical mass to engage in a number of different activities.

He consults with the local schools, different community groups and associations and plans a fun event in a local park with local coaches providing the lead for each session. He brings in clubs from different sports, including walking, cycling, angling and karate. He organizes softball himself, encouraging families or streets to take part together.

He promotes incentives to come to the event in family and street groups to the school, local groups, community associations and shops.

He finds that family groups take part in different activities and a number of the clubs gain new members including a group of young people who would like to do BMX cycling, as well as road cycling.

The family/street softball event is a great success and it is planned to be played every month during the summer months.

Stop and consider

How does Peter make his coaching sessions accessible and appropriate to all ages? List the ways in the space provided below.

Feedback

Peter made his coaching session accessible and appropriate to all ages by:

- encouraging people to come in family groups
- providing low-impact sports, such as walking and angling
- not prescribing what people should do
- ensuring that everyone included in a new softball-related activity is at the same level
- distributing information to different outlets to attract all ages.

4.5 Economically Disadvantaged People

DON'T MAKE ASSUMPTIONS

- Don't assume that, just because not many people from disadvantaged backgrounds currently attend your coaching sessions, they simply aren't interested in your sport. Think back to the barriers to participation identified in Section 2.
- Remember, the reasons people participate in sport are the same, regardless of their personal circumstances (eg to have fun, improve fitness, make friends, as a personal challenge, for competition). The benefits of sport are also the same (eg improving confidence and self-esteem, handling pressure and stress).

COMMUNICATE

- Consult with other relevant bodies that will be able to guide you on how to assist in understanding issues such as:
    - appropriate venues, days and times for coaching sessions
    - specific requirements and issues related to the particular economic disadvantage
    - appropriate means of advertising your coaching sessions.
- Use language that is sensitive, appropriate and relevant both during and outside your coaching sessions (see Section 3.5 for more information).
- People from different economically disadvantaged backgrounds will not have different needs and aspirations to anyone else in sport. It is, therefore, important to consult with individuals to find out about:
    - any specific support or dispensation that is needed
    - what kind of support they will need from you
    - existing skills and fitness levels
    - what they hope to achieve from the coaching sessions
    - other issues (eg transport, costs).
- Advertise your coaching sessions adequately and appropriately – make sure any promotional material you produce includes information that is relevant to people who may have challenges in terms of their economic status.
- Encourage other coaches at your club to attend the sports coach UK workshop 'Equity in Your Coaching'. Workshop dates and locations are available from the Workshop Booking Centre.

See page 128 for contact details of the Workshop Booking Centre.

69

ACT APPROPRIATELY

• In order to create a positive, welcoming coaching environment, make sure you use language that is sensitive, appropriate and relevant, so as not to upset or offend people who are economically disadvantaged. It can be difficult to know what is acceptable and unacceptable – refer back to Section Three for guidance.

SEEK ADVICE

If in doubt, contact organisations that can offer help and advice.

See pages 141–154 for contact details.

Bear the information in the panels in mind as you complete the activity on the next page.

© Action Images/Reuters

ACTIVITY 7

Scenario 23

Melvin and Heather run a local basketball club for adults and young people.

The adult club has a number of established players, some of whom have been made redundant from a local factory, and one new player who is at university.

Local schools provide the junior players, some of whom have to travel on two buses to get to training and matches. However, some of the players in both senior and junior age groups are from more affluent areas and drive to and from matches and training.

Melvin and Heather call a meeting of all players and raise the issue of different economic circumstances. Following a long discussion, they decide to have three membership categories:

• employed players

• unemployed players

• students and under-16s.

One of the parents also offers to develop some fund-raising by making an application to Awards for All, agrees to organise a meeting with the local authority and seeks the forms for applications to the local sports council and the regional SportsAid contact.

Another adult coming from outside of town arranges with three players to pick them up on the way to practice.

Stop and consider

How have Melvin and Heather made the club more accessible to people from economically disadvantaged backgrounds? List the ways in the space provided below.

Feedback

Melvin and Heather addressed the issues of socioeconomic status by:

• discussion with all the players regarding the situation, so everyone was clear about the differing situations

• ensuring more people took responsibility for raising income that will benefit all members

• ensuring the club has different membership systems for people with different economic circumstances

• arranging to share lifts, enabling the players who have the least money to save.

© Alan Edwards

4.6 Lesbian, Gay, Bisexual and Transgender People

▶ DON'T MAKE ASSUMPTIONS

- Don't assume that people attending your coaching sessions are not lesbian, gay, bisexual or transgender. Think back to the barriers to participation identified in Section 2.6.

- Remember, the reasons people participate in sport are the same (eg to have fun, improve fitness, make friends, as a personal challenge, for competition), no matter what their sexual orientation. The benefits of sport are also the same (eg improving confidence and self-esteem, handling pressure and stress). Try to raise awareness of these benefits – if possible, use lesbian, gay, bisexual or transgender people as positive role models.

▶ COMMUNICATE

- Consult with lesbian, gay, bisexual or transgender people, or relevant organisations, about issues such as:
  - appropriate venues, days and times for coaching sessions
  - specific needs and aspirations lesbian, gay, bisexual and transgender people may have
  - appropriate means of advertising your coaching sessions.

Doing this will prove to lesbian, gay, bisexual and transgender people that you are serious about encouraging them to join your coaching sessions.

- Use language that is sensitive, appropriate and relevant both during and outside your coaching sessions (see Section 3.6 for more information).

- Lesbian, gay, bisexual or transgender people will have different needs and aspirations. It is, therefore, important to consult with individuals to find out about:
  - any specific requirements
  - what kind of support they will need from you
  - their existing skills and fitness levels
  - what they hope to achieve from the coaching sessions
  - other issues (eg transport, costs).

- Advertise your coaching sessions adequately and appropriately – make sure any promotional material you produce includes information that is relevant to lesbian, gay, bisexual and transgender people.

- Encourage other coaches at your club to attend the sports coach UK workshop 'Equity in Your Coaching'. Workshop dates and locations are available from the Workshop Booking Centre.

See page 128 for contact details of the Workshop Booking Centre.

ACT APPROPRIATELY

• In order to create a positive, welcoming coaching environment, make sure you use language that is sensitive, appropriate and relevant, so as not to upset or offend lesbian, gay, bisexual and transgender people. It can be difficult to know what is acceptable and unacceptable – refer back to Section Three for guidance.

SEEK ADVICE

If in doubt, contact organisations that can offer help and advice.

See pages 141–154 for contact details.

Bear the information in the panels in mind as you complete the activity on the next page.

© Alan Edwards

ACTIVITY 8

Read through the following scenario. As you do, try to identify if the local authority is promoting its services to lesbian, gay, bisexual and transgender people sensitively and appropriately.

Scenario 24

The local authority have planned to promote a gay and lesbian games to improve access to sports clubs and societies for people who are lesbian, gay, bisexual and transgender. The planning group talks to national groups representing lesbian, gay, bisexual and transgender people to ensure that the event is promoted sensitively and appropriately. The planning group involves local representatives of these national groups and also advertises for people to become members of the planning group.

The event is planned at a weekend and is linked to a broader festival and is organized by local people who wish to celebrate their sexuality. The event has a series of sports with 'come and try it' sessions run by local clubs who are also seeking to increase membership.

The event is advertised nationally in appropriate media to attract lesbian, gay, bisexual and transgender people to the event. Locally, it is advertised on the advice of the planning group and proves a great success, with many people joining local clubs. The clubs are selected as those who have achieved or are aiming to achieve Club Mark and have proved that they do not discriminate on any grounds.

Stop and Consider

How has the Local Authority increased the opportunities for people who are Gay, Lesbian, Bisexual and Transgender? List the ways in the space provided below.

Feedback

The planning group addressed opening access to sports clubs by lesbian, gay, bisexual and transgender people by:

• involving people from within the community to assist in planning and promoting the event
• ensuring that any continuation of participation is delivered in clubs that do not discriminate on the groups of sexuality
• promoting the event through appropriate media outlets that would give a positive image of the event
• consulting with national agencies to ensure they positively promoted the event
• communicating effectively with the target audience.

4.7 Summary

This section has identified ways to make your coaching sessions more accessible and appropriate for the key target groups. General points that apply to all the groups are shown in the diagram on the next page.

However, despite your best efforts to ensure that your coaching sessions are as equitable as possible, you cannot guarantee that everyone who attends them will behave in an equitable way. Section Five provides guidance on how to challenge instances of inequitable behaviour that could arise during your coaching sessions.

© Action Images/Reuters

Coach

DON'T MAKE ASSUMPTIONS ABOUT:

- which sports people are interested in
- which sports people are able to do
- people's reasons for taking part in sport – these are usually the same, regardless of ability, ethnic group, gender, age, background or sexuality
- people's reasons for not taking part in sport – just because you may not currently coach many people from the key target groups doesn't mean they aren't interested in your sport.

COMMUNICATE

- Consult people from the key target groups about their needs and aspirations.
- Consult organisations that can help you meet the needs of the key target groups.
- Use language that is sensitive, appropriate and relevant.
- Advertise your coaching sessions adequately, appropriately and in the right places.
- Encourage other coaches at your club to attend workshops relating to equity issues.

CATER FOR DIFFERENT NEEDS

- Understand the barriers to participation that may put people off attending your coaching sessions.
- Be aware of the needs and aspirations of people from the key target groups.
- Identify safety and medical issues.
- Hold your coaching sessions at convenient venues and times.
- Keep the cost of your coaching sessions as low as possible.

SEEK ADVICE

Contact organisations that can offer help and advice.

See pages 141–154 for contact details.

Participation

Section 5

Challenging Inequitable Behaviour

5.0 What's In It For You?

As a coach, you not only have a responsibility to behave equitably yourself, but you also play an important role in promoting equitable behaviour among your participants. It is important to recognise that, despite your best efforts to be a good role model, incidents of inequitable behaviour may arise during your coaching sessions.

By the end of this section, you should be able to:

• anticipate the kind of inequitable behaviour that could arise in your coaching sessions

• select appropriate ways of dealing with it.

Challenging inequitable behaviour doesn't mean adopting the role of 'equity police' and judging participants' behaviour. Remember, people may not be aware that the way they are behaving is unacceptable. Your role is to raise participants' awareness of sports equity issues and help them become more equitable.

5.1 Anticipating Inequitable Behaviour

Inequitable behaviour can be verbal, written or physical. Examples of each type are shown in the table below.

Type of Inequitable Behaviour	Examples
Verbal	• Racist, sexist or homophobic language • Ridicule or bullying because of a personal characteristic (eg wearing glasses, being disabled)
Written	• All of the above written down in some way (eg graffiti, in a letter, text messages on a mobile phone)
Physical	• Action taken against somebody because of their race, gender, personal characteristics, sexuality. Examples include: – pushing – biting – tripping somebody up and pretending it was an accident – touching somebody inappropriately – stealing or destroying other people's property – excluding somebody from taking part in an activity.

Inequitable behaviour can have a profound effect on the individual or groups of people it is directed against. This is highlighted in the example below.

Points of interest

In November 2000, the NSPCC published the results of major research[1] carried out to explore the childhood experience of young people in the UK, including their experience of abuse and neglect. The survey found that:

• 43% of the young people questioned identified bullying or being discriminated against by other children as the most common source of distress and misery

• bullying occurred mostly because of personal characteristics such as size, dress, race or manner of speech

• name-calling and verbal abuse were the most common forms of bullying

• 14–15% of the young people questioned were physically attacked

• many reported having had their property stolen or damaged.

The report concludes that, for many children, the wider world of school, friends and community contains threats of bullying and discrimination and, for girls in particular, sexual harassment and violence.

Although it would be impossible to account for every eventuality, anticipating the kind of inequitable behaviour that could arise during your coaching sessions will mean you are better prepared to deal with any incidences that may occur. The next activity asks you to identify examples of inequitable behaviour from a list of coaching scenarios.

[1] NSPCC (2000) *Child Maltreatment in the United Kingdom: A Study of the Prevalence of Child Abuse and Neglect.* London: NSPCC.

ACTIVITY 9

1 Read through the following scenarios and decide which are examples of equitable and inequitable behaviour. Put a tick in the appropriate column to indicate your response.

2 If you decide a scenario is an example of inequitable behaviour, note what type it is – verbal, written or physical.

Scenario	Equitable	Inequitable
1 You are coaching a group of men and you hear one player telling the rest of the team that they are useless and playing like a bunch of girls.		
2 You find out that one of the children you coach has received a note signed by other team members, telling her she's no longer wanted on the team because she's too fat.		
3 One of the players you coach scores a good goal and is congratulated by the rest of the team.		
4 You coach both men and women at your club. You notice that every time you coach two of the younger women, several of the men watch and make comments about the way they are dressed and other suggestive comments, which the women obviously find upsetting.		
5 You are told that some lesbian participants who attend your coaching sessions are frequently heard telling some of the young girls at the club that men are 'no good' and that they 'can't be trusted'.		
6 A member of the team you coach has not been involved in the sport for long. Other team members are supportive and always react positively to the efforts of the new member, even if it sometimes means they lose possession of the ball.		

Scenario	Equitable	Inequitable
7 Several of your club's members are from ethnic minorities. One day, one of these members draws your attention to a poster on the coaching notice board, which has been defaced with racist graffiti. You are given the name of the perpetrators, one of whom is a star player at the club.		
8 After a training session, you enter a changing room to see several young participants taunting another participant who wears glasses. One person even takes his glasses from him and stands on them.		
9 When asked to vote for the Player of the Year Award, the team you coach vote for a club member who is not the best player in the team, but is reliable, supportive and always turns up for training.		
10 You hear one of your participants telling another participant that he is playing 'like a spastic'.		

Feedback

Compare your answers with those provided below:

	Scenario	Equitable	Inequitable
1	You are coaching a group of men and you hear one player telling the rest of the team that they are useless and playing like a bunch of girls.		✓ Verbal
2	You find out that one of the children you coach has received a note signed by other team members, telling her she's no longer wanted on the team because she's too fat.		✓ Written
3	One of the players you coach scores a good goal and is congratulated by the rest of the team.	✓	
4	You coach both men and women at your club. You notice that every time you coach two of the younger women, several of the men watch and make comments about the way they are dressed and other suggestive comments, which the women obviously find upsetting.		✓ Verbal
5	You are told that some lesbian participants who attend your coaching sessions are frequently heard telling some of the young girls at the club that men are 'no good' and that they 'can't be trusted'.		✓ Verbal
6	A member of the team you coach has not been involved in the sport for long. Other team members are supportive and always react positively to the efforts of the new member, even if it sometimes means they lose possession of the ball.	✓	

Scenario	Equitable	Inequitable
7 Several of your club's members are from ethnic minorities. One day, one of these members draws your attention to a poster on the coaching notice board, which has been defaced with racist graffiti. You are given the name of the perpetrators, one of whom is a star player at the club.		✔ Written
8 After a training session, you enter a changing room to see several young participants taunting another participant who wears glasses. One person even takes his glasses from him and stands on them.		✔ Physical
9 When asked to vote for the Player of the Year Award, the team you coach vote for a club member who is not the best player in the team, but is reliable, supportive and always turns up for training.	✔	
10 You hear one of your participants telling another participant that he is playing 'like a spastic'.		✔ Verbal

5.2 Dealing with Inequitable Behaviour

You should always challenge inequitable behaviour in a positive way. The panel below provides some useful points to bear in mind.

Points of interest

- Having a code of practice will make it easier to deal with inequitable behaviour (eg being able to suspend or expel participants for unacceptable behaviour). Establish a code of practice that is part of the conditions of membership of your club or team. This could include things such as:
  - treating each other with respect
  - not using racist or sexist language
  - praising effort
  - not bullying or ridiculing other participants
  - acting sensitively with regard to the feelings of others.

- Avoid confrontation.
- Select the most appropriate time and place to challenge inequitable behaviour (eg discreetly during breaks or directly in front of the rest of the group).
- Act as you would want participants to act (ie be a good role model).
- Use language that is relevant, sensitive and appropriate.
- Devise a way to punish persistent offenders (eg suspend or fine players who break the code of practice).
- Devise a way to reward fair play and equitable behaviour.
- Point out that just because a team member doesn't appear to mind being referred to in an inequitable way, not everyone else will put up with it.

The next activity takes the examples of inequitable behaviour from Activity 9 and asks you to think about how you would deal with them.

ACTIVITY 10

Re-read the following examples of inequitable behaviour and make a note of how you would deal with them in the right-hand column. Don't worry if you find this difficult – some suggestions are provided on page 88.

Scenario	How to Deal With It
1 You are coaching a group of men and you hear one player telling the rest of the team that they are useless and playing like a bunch of girls.	
2 You find out that one of the children you coach has received a note signed by other team members, telling her she's no longer wanted on the team because she's too fat.	
3 You coach both men and women at your club. You notice that every time you coach two of the younger women, several of the men watch and make comments about the way they are dressed and other suggestive comments, which the women obviously find upsetting.	

Scenario	How to Deal With It
4 You are told that some lesbian participants who attend your coaching sessions are frequently heard telling some of the young girls at the club that men are 'no good' and that they 'can't be trusted'.	
5 Several of your club's members are from ethnic minorities. One day, one of these members draws your attention to a poster on the coaching notice board, which has been defaced with racist graffiti. You are given the names of the perpetrators, one of whom is a star player at the club.	
6 After a training session, you enter a changing room to see several young participants taunting another participant who wears glasses. One person even takes his glasses from him and stands on them.	
7 You hear one of your participants telling another participant that he is playing 'like a spastic'.	

Now turn over.

Feedback

The table below contains suggested ways of dealing with the examples of inequitable behaviour in Activity 10. These are by no means the only methods – you may well have come up with others that would be more appropriate for your coaching situation.

Scenario	*How to Deal With It*
1 You are coaching a group of men and you hear one player telling the rest of the team that they are useless and playing like a bunch of girls.	• Take the participant to one side and suggest that this is not an appropriate way to talk because it implies that women are not as good at sport as men. It is also not positive to tell a group they are useless. Remind the participant of the club's code of practice. • Alternatively, talk to the whole group and ask them how they felt about being spoken to in that way and, more importantly, how they think women would have felt if they had overheard what was said.
2 You find out that one of the children you coach has received a note signed by other team members, telling her she's no longer wanted on the team because she's too fat.	• Speak to the team as a whole (and their parents or carers, if relevant) and tell them you have found out that some unfair behaviour has been going on, which has upset one team member in particular. Say how disappointed you are with their behaviour and that, unless it stops, you may have to take further action (eg cancelling a tournament or trip to see a professional game). • Speak to the child who received the note (and perhaps a parent or carer). Make it clear that you support her and try to boost her self-esteem.
3 You coach both men and women at your club. You notice that every time you coach two of the younger women, several of the men watch and make comments about the way they are dressed and other suggestive comments, which the women obviously find upsetting.	• Speak to the men and point out that they are breaking the club's code of practice and upsetting the women involved. • If the men continue to behave inequitably, you could exclude or suspend them (if this is allowed under your club constitution or code of practice).

Scenario	How to Deal With It
4 You are told that some lesbian participants who attend your coaching sessions are frequently heard telling some of the young girls at the club that men are 'no good' and that they 'can't be trusted'.	• Talk to the women and ask them to keep their opinions to themselves. Point out that their language is sexist and not acceptable. • Remind them of the club's code of practice and ask them to try to act in a positive way by supporting the male club members.
5 Several of your club's members are from ethnic minorities. One day, one of these members draws your attention to a poster on the coaching notice board, which has been defaced with racist graffiti. You are given the names of the perpetrators, one of whom is a star player at the club.	• Establish whether or not the names you have been given are correct. • Talk to the participants involved and point out that their actions are racist and will not be tolerated at the club. You could also tell them that they could be suspended or thrown out of the club because of their behaviour (if this is allowed under your club constitution or code of practice). • The fact that one of the perpetrators is a star player should not affect the way you act, unless you use it to emphasise that he is a role model for other club members and should therefore act equitably. • Ask the perpetrators to post a written apology on the notice board and to make a verbal apology to the club members from ethnic minorities. • If you are unable to establish who the perpetrators are, speak to the club as a whole, highlighting the club's code of practice and the action that could be taken against those who go against it. You could also put up posters reminding players of their responsibility to act in an equitable way towards each other.

Scenario	How to Deal With It
6 After a training session, you enter a changing room to see several young participants taunting another participant who wears glasses. One person even takes his glasses from him and stands on them.	• Speak to the team as a whole (and, if relevant, their parents or carers) and let them know you have found out that some inequitable behaviour has been going on, which has upset one team member in particular. • Say how disappointed you are with their behaviour and that, unless it stops, you may have to take further action (eg cancelling a tournament or trip to see a professional game). You could suspend the participant who stood on the glasses (if this is allowed under your club constitution or code of practice). • Speak to the participant who was on the receiving end of the taunts (and his parent or carer, if relevant). Make it clear that you support him and try to boost his self-esteem.
7 You hear one of your participants telling another participant that he is playing 'like a spastic'.	• Speak to the participant individually. • Point out that his language is unacceptable because it: — is wrong to refer to a person with cerebral palsy as a spastic — implies that somebody with a disability is less capable of taking part in sport than somebody without. • Remind him of the club's code of practice.

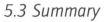

5.3 Summary

You should now feel more comfortable about dealing with inequitable behaviour. Remember, this doesn't mean adopting the role of 'equity police' and judging participants' behaviour, but raising awareness of equity issues and helping participants become more equitable. Doing so will help to create a safe and enjoyable sporting environment for everyone.

Try to set a good example and promote good practice at all times. Doing so not only encourages your participants to behave appropriately, it also ensures the way you coach is equitable and protects you from allegations that could otherwise be made against you. Failure to act in an equitable way not only constitutes poor coaching practice – in some instances, it may even be against the law. Section Six looks at the sources of liability that may affect coaches.

Section 6

Legal Framework Affecting Equity

6.0 What's In It For You?

As described in Section One, providing sporting opportunities for everyone in society is not just a moral responsibility, but could also be a legal requirement in some instances, particularly for organisations deemed to be service providers (eg local authorities, governing bodies of sport, sporting organisations).

Whether you are an employed or voluntary coach, it is important that you are aware of the legal framework that affects equity. This section will introduce you to three sources of liability with which all coaches should be familiar:

- Discrimination (Section 6.1)
- Negligence (Section 6.2)
- Defamation (Section 6.3).

6.1 Discrimination

Points of interest

What is Discrimination?

Discrimination is the action people take on the basis of their prejudices. It occurs when a prejudiced person has the power to put their prejudices into action, which results in unfair and unjust treatment. There are two types of discrimination:

• **Direct discrimination** occurs when someone is treated worse than other people in the same or a similar situation.

• **Indirect discrimination** occurs when there is a rule or condition that applies to everybody, but people from a certain group are unable to meet it and there is no justifiable reason for having that rule.

This section provides a brief overview of the key discrimination-related legislation you need to be aware of:

• Equal Pay Act 1970 Equal Value (Amendment) Regulations 1983
• Rehabilitation of Offenders Act 1974
• Sex Discrimination Act 1975, 1986 and 1999
• Race Relations Act 1976, Amendment Act 2000
• Employment Protection (Consolidation) Act 1978
• Children Act 1989 and 2004
• Disability Discrimination Act 1995 and 2004
• Race Relations (Northern Ireland) Order 1997
• Northern Ireland Act 1998
• Scotland Act 1998
• Human Rights Act 1998
• Employment Equality (Sexual Orientation) Regulations 2003
• Employment Equality (Religion and Belief) Regulations 2003
• Disability Discrimination Act 2005
• Equality Act 2006
• Employment Equality (Age) Regulations 2006

Positive Action or Positive Discrimination

As identified above, all discrimination is illegal. However, the difference between positive action and positive discrimination is sometimes misinterpreted. Positive action is action taken to address an inequality. For example, the provision of women-only coach education courses is positive action if women are under-represented in coaching. Positive discrimination would be an action that discriminates against a particular group to benefit another group.

Legislation, as identified in Section One, is in place to make sure that people are not discriminated against in the workplace and while accessing services. The aim of this section is to help you understand how these key Acts could affect your coaching practice.

Sex Discrimination Act 1975, 1986 and 1999

The Sex Discrimination Act 1975 applies to England, Northern Ireland, Scotland and Wales. The underlying principle of the Sex Discrimination Act 1975 is that men and women should be treated equally. Section 29 of the Act requires equality in the provision of goods, facilities and services to the public or a section of the public, whether for payment or not.

When passing the Act, however, Parliament decided there should be exceptions to the general rule of equal treatment in special circumstances. The sections of the Act that are particularly relevant to the sport and leisure industry are summarised below:

• Section 35 (1) c) allows facilities or services to be restricted to one sex if it can be demonstrated that they are such that users of one sex are:

  – more likely to suffer serious embarrassment at the presence of the opposite sex

 or

  – likely to be in a state of undress and might reasonably object to the presence of users of the opposite sex.

• Section 35 (2) permits single-sex provision If physical contact is likely between users of the opposite sex and there might be a reasonable objection to this.

• Section 34 permits voluntary groups of various kinds to cater for one sex only. Such organisations may restrict membership, benefits and facilities to one sex and may provide public services to one sex only.

Sexual harassment is a form of sexual discrimination. It is unwanted, often sexual attention and may include:

• written or verbal abuse or threats

• sexually oriented comments

• jokes, lewd comments or sexual innuendos

• taunts about body, dress, marital status or sexuality

• shouting and/or bullying

• ridiculing or undermining of performance or self-respect

• sexual or homophobic graffiti

• practical jokes based on sex

• intimidating sexual remarks, invitations or familiarity

• domination of meetings, training sessions or equipment

• condescending or patronising behaviour

• physical contact, fondling, pinching or kissing

• sex-related vandalism

• offensive telephone calls or photos

• bullying on the basis of sex.

Text reproduced with the kind permission of WomenSport International from their leaflet *Sexual Harassment and Abuse of Girls and Women in Sport.*

For further information on the Sex Discrimination Act 1975 and related issues, contact the Equal Opportunities Commission (until the establishment of the Commission for Equality and Human Rights) (see page 158 for contact details).

Implications for You

At present in the UK, there are very few examples of legal proceedings that have been brought against coaches under the Sex Discrimination Act 1975. However, this is not to say it couldn't happen. The panel below shows an example of action taken against sex discrimination in football.

Hardwick v The Football Association

In 1997, Vanessa Hardwick successfully claimed that The FA sexually discriminated against her on a two-week coaching course. Her case was backed by the Equal Opportunities Commission. She complained that the course had been dominated by men, that she had been deliberately left out of certain role-plays and that, despite achieving better marks than a number of men who had passed an earlier course, she was failed.

The tribunal decided that The FA had deliberately failed her on the grounds that she was a woman and she was awarded £5000 for injury to feelings. The tribunal requested that she be awarded the coaching qualification or receive further damages.

Two years later, the tribunal ruled that Hardwick should receive £16000 compensation for potential loss of earnings and recommended that she be awarded her Advanced Coaching Licence within 28 days.

In order to promote best practice when working with mixed-gender groups, you should:

- always assess participants on the basis of their ability, not gender
- have an open mind and no preconceived ideas about women's and girls' abilities, and always treat everyone fairly
- try to develop team-selection criteria based on ability, and always be able to provide written comments to justify your decision to select particular participants
- try to involve team captains or others when selecting teams, to avoid any biased decisions
- use language which is sensitive, appropriate and relevant
- ensure appropriate facilities are available to accommodate all participants' needs.

These are just some of the things to bear in mind when coaching women and girls – refer back to Section Four for further guidance.

The following organisations can offer further advice and support on working with women and girls:

• Equality Commission for Northern Ireland
• Equal Opportunities Commission (until the establishment of the Commission for Equality and Human Rights)
• Women's Sports Foundation

See page 151 for contact details.

Race Relations Act 1976

The Race Relations Act 1976 applies to England, Scotland and Wales, but not Northern Ireland (see overleaf for the Northern Ireland equivalent). It gives anyone who thinks they may have been discriminated against on racial grounds (ie because of their race, colour, nationality, or ethnic or national origin) the right to seek justice in the courts or an employment tribunal. It covers the following areas:

• education
• employment
• housing
• provision of goods, facilities and services
• training.

The Act deals with people's discriminatory actions and the effect of their actions. Motives do not matter, but if someone's attitude is proven to be racist, as well as their actions being discriminatory, this will count against them in any court or tribunal.

Racist abuse and harassment (eg insensitive language, persistent remarks) are forms of racial discrimination.

Points of interest

Note that incidents in public places, such as racial abuse in the street or at a football match, are not covered by the Race Relations Act. These are dealt with under the Public Order Act and the Football Offences Act respectively.

Race Relations (Amendment) Act 2000

The Race Relations (Amendment) Act 2000 is the first major reform of the Race Relations Act 1976 and aims to provide wider protection against racial discrimination. The Act amends the 1976 Act in two main ways:

- It makes it unlawful for any public authority, in relation to any of its activities, to discriminate on racial grounds whether directly, indirectly or by victimisation[1]. This applies not only to statutory bodies (eg local authorities), but also to any private or voluntary body when carrying out public functions.

- It makes it a duty for all public authorities to have due regard to the need to eliminate racial discrimination and to promote racial equality.

> For further information on the Race Relations Act 1976 and Race Relations (Amendment) Act 2000, and related issues, contact the Commission for Racial Equality until the establishment of the Commission for Equality and Human Rights (see page 160 for contact details).

Disability Discrimination Act 1995 and 2004

The Disability Discrimination Act 1995 applies to England, Northern Ireland, Scotland and Wales. Part III of the Disability Discrimination Act 1995 makes it unlawful for people who provide goods, facilities or services to the public (service providers) to discriminate against disabled people.

Service providers must treat disabled people in the same way they would treat other people when offering a service or facility, whether for payment or not. In addition, they must make all reasonable adjustments to the environment in which they operate, to accommodate an individual's impairment.

This involves:

- changing any policies, practices and procedures that might discriminate against disabled people
- providing auxiliary aids and services
- providing their services by a reasonable alternative means, if there is a physical barrier to access.

In 2004, the final stage of implementing Part III of the Act was introduced. Since 1 October 1999, sports clubs have had to make reasonable adjustments for disabled people, such as providing extra help, or making changes to the way they provide their services.

From 1 October 2004, sports clubs have had to make other reasonable adjustments in relation to the physical features of their premises, to overcome physical barriers to access.

Discrimination occurs when a disabled person is treated less favourably than someone else and this treatment:

- is for a reason relating to the person's disability and that reason does not apply to the other person
- cannot be justified.

[1] See the racial discrimination entry in Appendix A for definitions of these terms.

Unlawful discrimination occurs when a service provider discriminates by:

• refusing to serve a disabled person

• offering a disabled person a lower standard of service

• offering a disabled person less favourable terms

• failing to make alterations to a service or facility, which makes it impossible or unreasonably difficult for a disabled person to use.

Abuse and harassment (eg insensitive language, persistent remarks) are forms of disability discrimination.

> • Appendix D contains some useful suggestions on providing services to disabled people. Although not specifically aimed at coaches, you will, nonetheless, find them useful.
>
> • For further information on the Disability Discrimination Act 1995 and related issues, contact the Disability Rights Commission (see page 159 for contact details).

Implications for You

In order to promote best practice when deciding whether to involve disabled people in your coaching sessions, you should:

• always assess participants on the basis of their ability, not disability

• have an open mind and no preconceived ideas about what level of performance you think a particular participant is capable of

• advertise your coaching sessions in the right places (ie places that disabled people attend)

• find out if your governing body of sport has any recommendations on how to involve disabled people in your coaching sessions

• establish if you would need specialist equipment

• find out about workshops/courses you could attend to improve your knowledge of coaching disabled people.

As awareness of the DDA grows, so more cases will progress through the legal process. Some of the early examples of cases include:

Golf

Vernon Roper, who has multiple sclerosis, was refused permission by his local golf club to use a motorised golf cart, apparently on the basis that to do so would lead to irreparable damage to the turf. In particular, it was suggested by the golf club that the turf had only recently been laid and that until it had a chance to settle, there was no prospect of the client being allowed to use a motorised cart.

The court decided that the golf course unlawfully discriminated against the claimant by failing to discharge its legal duty to make an adjustment to allow the client to make use of its services. A reasonable adjustment was for the defendant to allow the claimant to use his golf buggy on the course in dry weather conditions. Health and safety concerns did not make the adjustment requested unreasonable, nor did they justify the failure to make the reasonable adjustment.

Rugby

The client, who is a wheelchair user, alleged unfavourable treatment by a rugby ground in its provisions for disabled fans. Rugby union rules state that a disabled person must be accompanied by a non-disabled person. This rule means that the client must purchase two tickets for each game he wishes to attend, although the one for his companion is at a reduced rate. In addition, although the client joined the rugby union's disabled fans register, he was not offered seating on the terrace, since the union's rule was that this was prioritised for those who had a disability as a result of playing rugby.

The rugby ground owners have agreed to change almost all of their ticketing policies and redesign their various forms. They are developing new policies, which they will agree with the DRC as part of a final settlement. They have also agreed to train all staff in disability equality.

sports coach UK workshops

• How to Coach Disabled People in Sport (Coaching Essentials Workshop)
• Coaching Disabled Performers (Develop Your Coaching Workshop).

Workshop dates and locations are available from the Workshop Booking Centre.

See page 128 for contact details of the Workshop Booking Centre.

Governing body sport-specific courses

Many governing bodies of sport run courses designed to assist those working with disabled sportspeople. Find out what your governing body of sport has to offer.

These are just some of the things to bear in mind when coaching disabled people – refer back to Section Four for further guidance.

The following organisations can offer further advice and support on working with disabled people:

• Disability Rights Commission

• Disability Sport Wales

• Disability Sports NI (DSNI)

• English Federation of Disability Sport (EFDS)

• local disability rights organisation (if one is available)

• local authority

• Royal National Institute for the Blind (RNIB)

• Scottish Disability Sport.

See pages 148–149 for contact details.

Race Relations (Northern Ireland) Order 1997

The Race Relations (Northern Ireland) Order is based on the Race Relations Act 1976 and became law in 1997. Section 21 of the Order makes it unlawful for people who provide goods, facilities or services to the public, or a section of the public, to discriminate on racial grounds against people seeking to obtain or use those goods, facilities or services by:

• refusing or deliberately omitting to provide them with goods, facilities or services

or

• refusing or deliberately omitting to provide them with goods, facilities or services of the same quality, in the same manner and on the same terms as other members of the public.

Section 38 of the Order relates specifically to sports and competitions. It outlines circumstances when discrimination on the basis of nationality or place of birth, or the length of time somebody has been resident in a particular area or place, is acceptable. This is only when:

• selecting one or more persons to represent a country, place or area, or any related association, in any sport or game

or

• abiding by the rules of any competition so far as they relate to eligibility to compete in any sport or game.

For further information on the Race Relations (Northern Ireland) Order 1997 and related issues, contact the Equality Commission for Northern Ireland (see page 159 for contact details).

Implications for You

At present in the UK, there are very few examples of legal proceedings that have been brought against coaches under the Race Relations Act 1976 or Race Relations (Northern Ireland) Order 1997. However, this is not to say that it couldn't happen. The panel below shows examples of action taken against racial discrimination in rugby league and football.

Rugby League

In October 2000, an employment tribunal found Super League club Leeds Rhinos guilty of 'unconscious racial discrimination'. It ruled that a black player was discriminated against when the head coach told him he would not get a first-team place 'irrespective of performance'. The head coach's comments were deemed 'ill-considered' and the club was accused of failing to adequately investigate the allegations of racial discrimination made by the player against the head coach.

Football

Although not as widespread as it was during the 1970s and 1980s, the problem of racism in football still exists. To help combat this, football authorities have begun to fine individual clubs for racial abuse committed by their fans towards opposition players from ethnic minorities (eg UEFA fined Red Star Belgrade £16000 for the racist behaviour of its fans towards black players in the Leicester City team during a UEFA Cup match in 2000). Rather than bringing charges of racial discrimination against individuals, football clubs are now held responsible for the behaviour of their fans.

In 2000, The Football Association (The FA) introduced a new set of disciplinary guidelines designed to clean up the image of English football. Within these, it specifies that clubs are responsible for crowd control and face fines or points deductions if fans behave in an unacceptable manner. In addition, any offence motivated by discrimination on racial grounds will result in double the usual penalty.

In order to promote best practice when working with participants from ethnic minorities, you should:

- always assess participants on the basis of their ability, not race
- have an open mind and no preconceived ideas about people from ethnic minorities, and always treat everyone fairly
- always use language that is sensitive, appropriate and relevant
- ensure that all participants behave appropriately during your coaching sessions and do not offend others.

These are just some of the things to bear in mind when coaching people from ethnic minorities – refer back to Section Four for further guidance.

The following organisations can offer further advice and support on working with people from ethnic minorities:

• Commission for Racial Equality (until the establishment of the Commission for Equality and Human Rights)

• Equal Opportunities Commission (until the establishment of the Commission for Equality and Human Rights)

• Equality Commission for Northern Ireland

• Sporting Equals.

See page 150 for contact details.

Northern Ireland Act 1998

Section 75 of the Northern Ireland Act 1998 states that, when carrying out their functions, all public bodies[1] must have due regard for the need to promote equality of opportunity between:

• persons of different religious belief, political opinion, racial group, age, marital status or sexual orientation

• men and women generally

• persons with a disability and persons without

• persons with dependants and persons without.

In addition, public bodies must promote good relations between people of different religious belief, political opinion or racial group, underpinned by three principles – equity, respecting diversity and interdependence.

In order to comply with Section 75 of the Northern Ireland Act 1998, all public bodies have been required to produce an Equality Scheme. This must highlight all their policies (both written and unwritten), procedures and practices. It must also include timescales by which all policies will be reviewed to ensure that everyone, regardless of their category, has equal access to their services.

---

[1] Public bodies are organisations such as district councils, health trusts, education and library boards, and non-departmental government agencies, such as the Sports Council for Northern Ireland, Arts Council, Probation Board for Northern Ireland and Water Service.

Scotland Act 1998

The Scotland Act 1998 gives the Scottish Parliament powers to promote equal opportunities for a broad range of groups and to encourage others to do so as well. The Act defines equal opportunities as:

...the prevention, elimination or regulation of discrimination between persons on grounds of sex or marital status, on racial grounds, or on grounds of disability, age, sexual orientation, language or social origin, or of other personal attributes, including beliefs or options, such as religious beliefs or political opinions.

Scotland Act 1998

The Scottish Executive has recognised that, while many communities live and work in harmony, some experience harassment, discrimination and exclusion. November 2000 saw the launch of its equality strategy, Working Towards Equality. Through this strategy, the Scottish Executive aims to work with people and organisations to:

• remove the causes of discrimination and prejudice

• strengthen and build on what is positive and inclusive

• promote a fair and just Scotland, where:

   – everyone has the opportunity to fulfil their potential in all areas of life

   – no-one is excluded

   – people respect each other and their differences.

Employment Equality (Sexual Orientation) Regulations 2003

Employment Equality (Religion and Belief) Regulations 2003

These sets of Regulations outlaw discrimination in employment and vocational training on the grounds of sexual orientation and religion and belief. They also outlaw direct and indirect discrimination, harassment and victimisation.

Disability Discrimination Act (DDA) 2005

In April 2005, a new Disability Discrimination Act was passed by Parliament, which amends or extends existing provisions in the DDA 1995, including:

• making it unlawful for operators of transport vehicles to discriminate against disabled people

• making it easier for disabled people to rent property and for tenants to make disability-related adaptations

• making sure that private clubs with 25 or more members cannot keep disabled people out, just because they have a disability

• extending protection to cover people who have HIV, cancer and multiple sclerosis from the moment they are diagnosed

• ensuring that discrimination law covers all the activities of the public sector

• requiring public bodies to promote equality of opportunity for disabled people.

www.direct.gov.uk/en/DisabledPeople/RightsAndObligations/DisabilityRights/DG_4001068

Employment Equality (Age) Regulations 2006

This set of Regulations outlaws discrimination in employment and vocational training on the grounds of age. It also outlaws direct and indirect discrimination, harassment and victimisation.

As the Regulations are relatively new, no cases have been enacted in relation to sport as yet.

Points of interest

Did You Know...?

Disability Discrimination Act 1995

1 The Disability Discrimination Act 1995 covers people:
- with physical impairments
- with learning disabilities
- whose mental health is impaired
- who use hearing aids

   ...but not people who wear glasses.

2 It is lawful to provide separate coaching sessions for disabled people, but unlawful to provide separate sessions for non-disabled people.

3 All sports facilities are legally required to provide auxiliary aids to enable disabled people to use them. Since 2004, they have also been legally required to make their premises accessible to disabled people.

Race Relations Act 1976

1 When selecting a team, or rules relating to eligibility to compete in a sport or game, it is sometimes lawful to discriminate on the basis of:
- nationality
- place of birth
- length of time lived in a particular area

   ...but unlawful to discriminate on the basis of:
- race or ethnic origin
- colour.

2 It is lawful to discriminate in the provision of separate training courses for sports staff (eg training for black people in leisure management).

3 It is unlawful for ethnic groups to set up their own sporting organisations and exclude people on the grounds of ethnic origin or national group.

Sex Discrimination Act 1975

1 In some circumstances, it is lawful to provide and advertise single-gender sports facilities.

2 It is unlawful to staff a women-only sports session with a male coach.

Based on information from Nottingham University (1999) 'Equality in Sport Means Quality Sport'. National Sports Development Seminar Facilitator's Pack.

6.2 Negligence

By far the most serious of the sources of liability explored in this resource would be a claim that a participant under your supervision had suffered injury, loss or damage because of your negligence as a coach. This section highlights the need for you to be aware of action that may be required of you during coaching sessions, to avoid instances of injury, loss or damage occurring, particularly when coaching disabled people.

There are four elements that together constitute a case for negligence:

• There exists a duty of care[1] towards the participant.
• This duty of care imposes a standard and negligence has caused that standard to be breached.
• The participant has suffered loss, harm, damage or injury.
• The breach of duty of care contributes to the loss, harm, damage or injury.

© Alan Edwards

[1] See pages 107–108 for further information about duty of care.

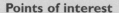

Points of interest

Duty of Care

As a coach, you have a duty to be:

Safe
- In any coaching environment where there is a forseeable risk of harm (this includes indoors, outdoors, wet and dry), you must carry out a risk assessment of the activity to be carried out within that environment and be able to provide documentary evidence to support that assessment.

- No-one can completely eliminate the risk of harm, but you must show evidence of having acted reasonably to minimise risks as far as humanly possible (eg safety of venue, equipment and playing surfaces).

- Make your participants fully aware of the risks involved in particular activities. This needs to be done repeatedly, clearly and thoroughly. Remember that a novice may not necessarily have the same comprehension or appreciation of the risks as an intermediate or expert participant.

- It is important to plan and deliver appropriate coaching sessions to meet the needs of your participants. This means selecting appropriate activities for the age, physical and emotional maturity, experience and ability of participants.

- Ensure participants are made aware of the health and safety guidelines which operate in your sport environment and within your governing body of sport.

- Reinforce and, if possible, practise emergency procedures.

- Encourage fair play and penalise incidences of foul play in your sport.

- Ensure participants stick to the rules and take as few risks as possible on their way to achieving their goals.

The sports coach UK Coaching Essentials workshop 'How to Coach Sport Safely' provides further information on ensuring the safety of your participants. Workshop dates and locations are available from the Workshop Booking Centre.

See page 128 for contact details of the Workshop Booking Centre.

Qualified
- To ensure your coaching is in line with the recommended good practice advocated by your governing body of sport and sports coach UK, you should obtain coaching qualifications. Governing bodies of sport can provide sport-specific training, while sports coach UK workshops and resources[1] provide general support and guidance that underpin coach education courses.

- Your coaching qualifications should be:
  - relevant
  - at the appropriate level
  - current and up to date.

---

[1] Further details available from sports coach UK and Coachwise 1st4sport (see page 128 for contact details).

Competent

- You should only coach those elements of your sport for which your training and competence is recognised by your governing body of sport.

- The National Occupational Standards for Coaching, Teaching and Instructing (and/or approved governing body of sport coaching awards) provide the framework for assessing competence at the different levels of coaching practice. Competence to coach should normally be verified through evidence of qualifications. Competence cannot be inferred solely from evidence of prior experience.

- You must be able to recognise and accept when to refer participants to other coaches or agencies. It is your responsibility, as far as possible, to verify the competence and integrity of any other person to whom you refer a participant.

- You should regularly seek ways of increasing your personal and professional development.

- You should welcome evaluation of your work by colleagues and be able to account for what you do and why to participants, employers, governing bodies of sport and colleagues.

- You have a responsibility to yourself and your participants to maintain your own effectiveness, resilience and abilities. You should recognise when your personal resources are so depleted that help is needed. This may necessitate the withdrawal from coaching temporarily or permanently.

Insured

- Insurance is essential for coaches, participants and sports providers (eg coaches, local authorities, governing bodies).

- Some governing bodies of sport do not allow coaches or participants to take part in their sport without insurance cover, while others include insurance as part of their affiliation fee. Check if your governing body operates an insurance scheme.

- sports coach UK Membership Services provides qualified coaches with insurance as part of its benefits package.

- Insurance should cover both public liability and personal accidents, and must be adequate for the risks faced in the particular sport.

Further information on the responsibilities of coaches is available in the:

- sports coach UK *Code of Practice for Sports Coaches*[1]

- National Occupational Standards for Coaching, Teaching and Instructing[2] – Section 7.3: Values Statement and Code of Ethics for Coaching, Teaching and Instructing.

[1] Available from Coachwise 1st4sport (see page 128 for contact details).

[2] Available from SkillsActive.

Negligence can be attributed both to your actions and your omissions. Injured participants have the right to sue coaches who may have caused injury by negligence. To do so, they would have to prove it was a breach of the standards demanded by the coach's duty of care that caused loss or injury. This is described as the 'but for' test:

But for the actions of the coach, would the loss or injury have occurred?

The following case study is an example of a court case brought by a disabled archer. It illustrates the duty of care you owe your participants.

Morrell v Owen and Others

In 1993, Mr Justice Mitchell adjudged that organisers and coaches of sporting activities owe a greater duty of care to disabled people than they would to non-disabled people.

The incident that brought about this judgment occurred during a training session held in 1993 by the British Amputee and Les Autres Sports Association (BALASA) in a sports hall in Birmingham. Two activities, archery and discus, were in progress in the same sports hall, which was divided by a fishnet curtain.

Miss Morrell, a disabled archer, was injured by a discus that struck the dividing curtain and hit her on the side of the head. The coaches present claimed they had warned Miss Morrell of the dangers of the activity at the other side of the curtain. Miss Morrell, however, claimed that she had not been warned. Mr Justice Mitchell believed Miss Morrell, stating that the kind of misthrow that occurred was entirely foreseeable, as was the accident in question. He stated that the coaches present owed a greater duty of care to the disabled people than they would to non-disabled people.

Implications for You

The Morrell v Owen and Others case illustrates how important it is for you to ensure that, when coaching disabled people, you take all the necessary measures to ensure your sessions are as safe as possible. You are strongly recommended to attend workshops/ courses to improve your knowledge of coaching disabled people. For example:

sports coach UK workshops:

• How to Coach Disabled People in Sport (Coaching Essentials Workshop)
• Coaching Disabled Performers (Develop Your Coaching Workshop)

Workshop dates and locations are available from the Workshop Booking Centre.

See page 128 for contact details of the Workshop Booking Centre.

Governing body sport-specific courses

Many governing bodies of sport run courses designed to assist those working with disabled sportspeople. Find out what your governing body of sport has to offer.

6.3 Defamation

Defamation is a statement that injures the reputation of another by exposing her to hatred, contempt or ridicule, or that tends to lower her in the esteem of right-thinking members of society.

There are two types of defamation:

• slander – the spoken word

• libel – the written word.

The following story illustrates defamation and describes a situation that could occur in any sports club at any level.

Alison is a coach at a local athletics club. She successfully applies to become part of the coaching team responsible for the elite squad at the club. Tushar is an up-and-coming member of the elite squad with potential to do well at the next regional athletics meeting. He is one of five athletes that Alison has specific responsibility for. However, Tushar finds it difficult to get on with Alison. She is always making derogatory remarks about him and purposefully ignores him during group coaching sessions, devoting more time to the other athletes. Tushar's performance consequently suffers and he misses out on a place in the club team.

Disappointed, Tushar asks to be moved to a different group with a different coach. Alison says that Tushar's poor form has nothing to do with her and that he should be more committed to his training if he wants to do well.

Tushar moves to a different group and is much happier. His performance improves dramatically and he comfortably wins the 100m final at the next regional athletics meeting. After the race, Alison is overheard telling her group of athletes that Tushar is selfish and attention seeking. She adds that she doesn't know how Tushar managed to do so well and that he must have taken performance-enhancing drugs to have made such a dramatic improvement in such a short space of time.

In the example above, Alison acted in an inappropriate and unprofessional manner, and could well have lost her position as coach at the athletics club. Make sure you never put yourself in a position where this could happen to you. Always set an example to your participants, in terms of behaviour and attitude. Your professional relationship with, and attitude towards, officials, spectators and other coaches must also be of the highest standard. Think about the influence your behaviour will have on your participants, their parents and other coaches. Try to be consistent and fair in what you say, what you do and what you ask of others.

6.4 Summary

This section should have helped you to understand the legal framework that affects equity. The key points you need to remember are listed in the panel over the page.

DISCRIMINATION

- Discrimination is the action people take on the basis of their prejudices. It occurs when a prejudiced person has the power to put their prejudices into action, which results in unfair and unjust treatment. There are two types of discrimination – direct and indirect.

- Key discrimination-related legislation includes:

  - Equal Pay Act 1970 Equal Value (Amendment) Regulations 1983
  - Rehabilitation of Offenders Act 1974
  - Sex Discrimination Act 1975, 1986 and 1999
  - Race Relations Act 1976, Amendment Act 2000
  - Employment Protection (Consolidation) Act 1978
  - Children Act 1989 and 2004
  - Disability Discrimination Act 1995 and 2004
  - Race Relations (Northern Ireland) Order 1997
  - Northern Ireland Act 1998
  - Scotland Act 1998
  - Human Rights Act 1998
  - Employment Equality (Sexual Orientation) Regulations 2003
  - Employment Equality (Religion and Belief) Regulations 2003
  - Disability Discrimination Act 2005
  - Equality Act 2006
  - Employment Equality (Age) Regulations 2006

- To avoid allegations of discrimination being made against you or your employer, always promote best practice when working with the key target groups.

NEGLIGENCE

- All coaches have a duty to be:

  - safe
  - qualified
  - competent
  - insured.

  This is known as duty of care.

- Negligence on the part of the coach causes a breach of duty and can result in a participant suffering injury, loss or damage.

- To avoid allegations of negligence being made against you, ensure you are aware of action that may be required of you during coaching sessions, particularly when coaching disabled people. Remember, negligence can be attributed both to your actions and your omissions.

DEFAMATION

- Defamation is a statement that injures the reputation of another by exposing him to hatred, contempt or ridicule, or that tends to lower him in the esteem of right-thinking members of society.

- There are two types of defamation:

  - slander – the spoken word
  - libel – the written word.

- To avoid allegations of defamation being made against you, always set an example to your participants, in terms of behaviour and attitude.

Section 7

Action Plan for Change

7.0 What's In It For You?

By now, you should appreciate just how vital it is to ensure that your coaching practice is as equitable as possible. But, however inspired you may feel to make improvements in the necessary areas, putting the theory into practice may seem rather daunting. Where do you start? To what extent should you aim to attract the key target groups to your coaching sessions?

By the end of this section, you should be able to:

• Identify areas you feel need improving or developing in your coaching practice

• explain why developing an equity policy is a good idea

• develop an action plan for adopting equity principles into your coaching practice.

7.1 Identifying Areas for Change

Before you can plan for change, you need to identify the areas you feel need improving or developing. The following ideas should help you do this:

- Use national population statistics as a general guide to gauge how equitable your coaching sessions are. However, remember that they only reflect the national average and that you also need to bear in mind the huge regional/local variations that can occur.

See pages 6–9 for further details.

- Ask another coach to observe one of your coaching sessions with particular reference to equity issues (eg the language you use). Compare their feedback with your own analysis of your coaching practice.

- Talk to your participants and find out whether anything you have said or done made them feel uncomfortable (you should already be doing this anyway as part of your session evaluations). Alternatively, you could devise a questionnaire for participants to fill in anonymously in their own time.

See Appendix G for a sample questionnaire.

- Find out if your governing body of sport has an equity policy. If so, get hold of a copy and make sure you follow its recommendations.

See Section 7.2 for further details about equity policies.

- Attend sports coach UK's 'Equity in Your Coaching' workshop and/or appropriate governing body of sport courses/workshops (see Appendix B for further details).
- Contact the organisations listed in Appendix B for help and advice.

7.2 Equity Statement and Policy

Assessing how equitable your coaching sessions currently are is the first stage towards ensuring they are accessible to everyone. It provides you with a starting point from which to measure your future achievements. The next stage is to demonstrate your commitment to equity.

sports coach UK has demonstrated its commitment by developing the following statement of intent:

sports coach UK is committed to the principles and practices of equal opportunities, both as an employer and in the delivery of services. Employment opportunities, programmes, products and services are available to all sections of the community and sports coach UK will not discriminate on grounds including, but not limited by, gender, race, disability, age, religious or political belief, sexual orientation, social background, ethnic origin, language, pregnancy, or marital or civil partnership status.

sports coach UK Equal Opportunities Statement of Intent
(taken from sports coach UK's Equity Policy)

Developing a similar equity statement for your club is a good way of raising awareness, both internally and externally, of your club's commitment to providing better sporting opportunities for the key target groups. It will also help you to:

• encourage more people to participate in your sport

• encourage more people into coaching, officiating and administrating in your sport

• improve your club's public image

• show that your club is responding to equity legislation and other equity-related initiatives.

As well as developing a general equity policy, you might want to create individual policies for each of the key target groups. For example, sports coach UK has developed a racial equality policy.

For an equity policy to work, everybody involved in your club (eg participants, coaches, employees, volunteers) needs to recognise that their own practice is perhaps not as equitable as it should be, and be prepared to do something about it. There also needs to be a commitment to implementing, monitoring and evaluating the policy, which may have implications for funding for new resources, equipment and training.

You may not personally be in a position to implement an equity policy – perhaps this would be the responsibility of club management or perhaps you are self-employed and coach at a variety of different venues. However, you still have a role to play in influencing the powers that be, as well as raising the awareness of participants, colleagues and other related groups about the importance of equity. There is also nothing to stop you developing your own personal equity policy to guide your coaching practice.

7.3 Putting the Theory into Practice

This resource may have highlighted specific areas in your own coaching practice that you feel you would like to improve or change altogether. Some things will be relatively easy to improve/change (eg being aware of the words and phrases you use). Other things may take a little longer and you may need to contact various organisations for assistance and advice. The next activity will help you focus on the improvements/changes required.

ACTIVITY 11

Stop and consider

What improvements or changes do you need to make to your coaching practice?

1. In the left-hand column of the table below, list the things you can change immediately or in the short term.

2. In the right-hand column, list the improvements and/or changes that might take longer to sort out. Some examples have been given to start you off.

Short-term Improvements/Changes	Long-term Improvements/Changes
Things I can change immediately: • *Use appropriate language and terminology so that I don't upset or offend participants.* • *Make sure I don't stereotype people, but am open-minded.*	*Things I can change in the long term:* • *Set up a coaching programme to encourage more people from local ethnic minorities to take part in my sport.* • *Encourage my club to provide better facilities for disabled people.*

3. Now that you have identified the short- and long-term improvements/changes that need to be made to your coaching practice, try to put an equity action plan together:

   a Select the three most important improvements/changes you listed in each column of the table above.

   b Use the blank action plans provided on pages 117–118 to help you identify:

   – how you intend to make each improvement/change

   – the date by which you intend to do it.

4. Review your action plans regularly and record your achievements. No doubt you will think of new improvements/changes to add to your list in the future.

A blank copy of the action plans is provided in Appendix H for you to photocopy and use as and when required.

SHORT-TERM IMPROVEMENTS/CHANGES

	What?	How?	When?
1			
2			
3			

LONG-TERM IMPROVEMENTS/CHANGES

	What?	How?	When?
1			
2			
3			

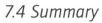

7.4 Summary

You should now have identified areas for improvement in your coaching practice and started to put together an equity action plan, whether it be specifically for your own coaching or for your club in general.

Working through this resource may have raised issues for you that you have never previously considered in your coaching. Part of being a good coach is being open to new ideas and training and, to some extent, being aware that you need updating in certain areas. It is also about understanding the needs of the people you are coaching and accepting advice on how to accommodate them. Section Eight provides a comprehensive list of useful contacts, references and recommended reading.

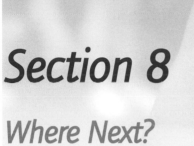

Section 8

Where Next?

8.0 Introduction

Part of being a good coach is being open to new ideas and training and, to some extent, being aware that you need updating in certain areas. It is also about understanding the needs of the people you are coaching and accepting advice on how to accommodate them. This section provides a comprehensive list of publications, workshops and organisations that can provide support and guidance on equity-related issues.

8.1 Further Reading/Workshops

This section lists a selection of useful publications and workshops that support the information provided in this resource. It is divided into subsections (one for each key target group, plus a miscellaneous section) to make it easier to find the resource(s) you are looking for.

Disabled People

Davis, R. (2002) *Inclusion Through Sports – A Guide to Enhancing Sport Experiences*. Champaign, Illinois, USA: Human Kinetics. ISBN: 978-0736034-39-5.

Disability Rights Commission (2005) 'Disability Discrimination Act 2005', www.drc-gb.org/pdf/DefnOfDisability.pdf

Disability Rights Commission (2006) 'The Disability Discrimination Act – Revised Guidance on the definition of disability', www.drc-gb.org/pdf/DefnOfDisability.pdf

English Federation of Disability Sport: 'Disability Sport Events', www.disabilitysport.org.uk/

English Federation of Disability Sport (2004) 'EFDS Count Me In: Development Framework (2004–2008)', www.efds.net/content/news/EFDS%20Brochure%20.pdf

For the latest disability sport news and research articles, log on to www.efds.net

For advice and guidance on the English Federation of Disability Sport's Inclusive Fitness Initiative (IFI) and to access audits for facilities, accessible fitness equipment, training and marketing, log on to www.inclusivefitness.org

Kerr, A. and Stafford, I. (2005) *How to Coach Disabled People in Sport*. Leeds: Coachwise Business Solutions. ISBN: 978-1-902523-54-5.

Kerr, A. and Stafford, I. (2005) *Coaching Disabled Performers*. Leeds: Coachwise Business Solutions. ISBN: 978-1-902523-60-6.

Leonard Cheshire and Scope (2006) 'Can-do Volunteering', www.can-do-volunteering.org/

Murray, P. (2002) *Hello! Are you listening? Disabled teenagers' experience of access to inclusive leisure*. London: Joseph Rowntree Foundation. ISBN: 978-1-842630-74-7

Royal National Institute for the Blind. (2005) *Fit for All: Including Children with Sight Problems in Sport*. Leeds: Coachwise Business Solutions. ISBN: 978-1-858786-44-5.

Scott Porter Research and Marketing Ltd (2000) 'Sport and People with a Disability: aiming at social inclusion' (research digest no 57), www.sportscotland.org.uk/ChannelNavigation/Resource+Library/Publications/Sport+and+People+with+a+Disability+Aiming+at+Social+Inclusion.htm

Shelley, P. (2002) *Everybody Here? Play and Leisure for Disabled Children and Young People*. London: Contact a Family. ISBN: 978-1874715-38-2.

Sport England (2000) 'Disability Survey 2000 – Young People with a Disability & Sport', www.sportengland.org/disability_young_people.pdf

Sport England (2002) 'Adults with a Disability and Sport National Survey 2000-2001', www.sportengland.org/adult_disability_full_report.pdf

Sport England (2005) 'Sport and Recreation for people with disabilities', www.sportengland.org/disability_booklet_apr_2005.pdf

Workshops

- **sports coach UK:**
  - Coaching Disabled Performers (Develop Your Coaching Workshop)
  - How to Coach Disabled People in Sport (Coaching Essentials Workshop)
- **English Federation of Disability Sport**:

  - Including Disabled Pupils in Physical Education

People from Ethnic Minorities

Asians in Football Forum (2005) 'Asians Can Play Football. Another Wasted Decade', www.cre.gov.uk/downloads/asianscanplayfootball.pdf

Commission for Racial Equality (1999) 'The Stephen Lawrence Inquiry – Implications for Racial Equality', www.cre.gov.uk/downloads/slinqlea.pdf

Commission for Racial Equality (2000) *Achieving Racial Equality: a standard for sport.* London: Commission for Racial Equality. ISBN: 978-1-854422-33-0.

Commission for Racial Equality (2002) 'Code of Practice on the Duty to Promote Race Equality', www.cre.gov.uk/downloads/duty_code.pdf

Commission for Racial Equality (2004) 'Goal Racial Equality in Football. Summary of research findings and action plan', www.cre.gov.uk/publs/cat_sport.html

Commission for Racial Equality (2004) 'Promoting Racial Equality through Sport. A Standard for local authorities, sport and leisure services', www.cre.gov.uk/downloads/prets.pdf

Commission for Racial Equality (2006) 'Complaints and Disciplinary Procedures. Sporting Equals Factsheet 11', www.cre.gov.uk/publs/cat_sport.html

Commission for Racial Equality (2006) 'Data Collection: Sporting Equals Factsheet 3', www.cre.gov.uk/publs/cat_sport.html

Commission for Racial Equality (2006) 'Developing Racial Equality Policies. Sporting Equals Factsheet 6', www.cre.gov.uk/publs/cat_sport.html

Commission for Racial Equality (2006) 'Developing Regional Racial Equality Sports Projects. Sporting Equals Factsheet 13', www.cre.gov.uk/publs/cat_sport.html

Commission for Racial Equality (2006) 'Employment and Ethnicity' (Factfile 1), www.cre.gov.uk/downloads/factfile01_employment_and_ethnicity.pdf

Commission for Racial Equality (2006) 'Positive Images in Sports Publicity: Sporting Equals Factsheet 1', www.cre.gov.uk/publs/cat_sport.html

Commission for Racial Equality (2006) 'Representation on Committees. Sporting Equals Factsheet 7', www.cre.gov.uk/publs/cat_sport.html

Commission for Racial Equality (2006) 'Working with Ethnic Minority Communities. Sporting Equals Factsheet 4', www.cre.gov.uk/publs/cat_sport.html

Ploszajski Lynch (2005) 'Increasing BME Participation in Sport & Physical Activity by Black and Ethnic Minority Communities', www.sportdevelopment.org.uk/menter_bmesports.pdf

Sport England (2000) 'Sports Participation and Ethnicity in England: national survey 1999/2000 headline findings', www.sportengland.org/text/ethnic_survey.pdf

Sporting Equals (2000) 'Racial Equality Charter', www.sportingequals.com/page_landing.asp?section=000100010006

Sporting Equals (2003) 'COI Communications Common Good Research. Ethnic Minority Communities', www.sportingequals.com/page.asp?section=0001000100080004&style=style_1

Sporting Equals (2005) 'Mapping of Ethnic Minority Communities in England. Birmingham, Sport Structures Ltd', www.sportingequals.com/page.asp?section=0001000100080004&style=style_1

Sporting Equals (2005) 'Identification of migrant, refugee and asylum seeker communities within England', www.sportingequals.com/page.asp?section=0001000100080004&style=style_1

Sporting Equals (2005) 'Identification of Workforce and Volunteer profiles within Sports Organisations', www.sportingequals.com/page.asp?section=0001000100080004&style=style_1

Sporting Equals (2005) 'Increasing BME Participation in Sport and Physical Activity by Black and Minority Ethnic Communities', www.sportingequals.com/page.asp?section=0001000100080004&style=style_1

Women's Sports Foundation UK (2006) 'Muslim women in sport: a minority within a minority', www.wsf.org.uk/documents/Muslim_women_in_Sport.pdf

Women and Girls

Biddle, S., Coalter, F., Donovan, T., MacBeth, J., Nevill, M. and Whitehead, S. (2005) 'Increasing Demand for Sport and Physical Activity by Girls', www.sportscotland.org.uk/ChannelNavigation/Resource+Library/Publications/Increasing+demand+for+sport+and+physical+activity+by+girls.htm

Equal Opportunities Commission (1997) 'A Guide to the Sex Discrimination Act 1975', www.womenandequalityunit.gov.uk/legislation/discrimination_act/sda-guide.pdf

Equal Opportunities Commission (2006) 'Women. Men. Different. Equal. Equal Opportunities Commission', www.eoc.org.uk/PDF/GED_CoP_Draft.pdf

Equal Opportunities Commission (no date) 'The Sex Discrimination Act and Equal Pay Act', www.eoc.org.uk/Default.aspx?page=15501

George Street Research (2004) 'Women in Sport Leadership', www.sportscotland.org.uk/ChannelNavigation/Resource+Library/Publications/Women+in+Sport+Leadership.htm

ISRM (undated) 'Single sex sport and leisure provision' (factsheet), www.isrm.co.uk/policy/PS003_singlesex.pdf

Sport England (2005) 'Determinants of sports and physical activity participation amongst 15-19-year-old young women in England', www.sportengland.org/15to19_women_full_report_final_24_nov_2005.doc

sports coach UK (2007) 'Women Into High Performance Coaching', www.sportscoachuk.org/About+Us/Policies/WHPC.htm

sportscotland and Women's Sport Foundation (2005) 'Making Women and Girls More Active: A Good Practice Guide', www.sportscotland.org.uk/ChannelNavigation/Resource+Library/Publications/Making+women+and+girls+more+active.htm

UK Sport (2003) 'UK Strategy Framework for Women and Sport', www.uksport.gov.uk/assets/File/Generic_Template_Documents/Standards_in_Sport/equity/StrategyandEquity_Nov03.pdf

UK Sport (2006) 'UK Strategy Framework for Women and Sport – Progress made towards objectives and targets set for 2005 and analysis of the current situation', www.uksport.gov.uk/pages/standards_in_sport_equity/

WomenSport International (no date) 'Sexual Harassment and Abuse of Girls and Women in Sport', www.sportsbiz.bz/womensportinternational/taskforces/wsi_position_statement.htm

Women's Sports Foundation (2000) 'WSF Products and Services', www.wsf.org.uk/products/index.php

Women's Sports Foundation UK (2004) 'Women, Girls Sport and Physical Activity – Evidence of Good Practice', www.wsf.org.uk/docs/WSF-Goodpractice.doc

Women's Sports Foundation UK (2005) 'Women, Girls Sport and Physical Activity – Barriers to Sport and Physical Activity', www.wsf.org.uk/docs/WSF-Barriers%5b1%5d.doc

Women's Sports Foundation UK (2006) 'Current UK Initiatives in Women's Sport', www.wsf.org.uk/informed/fact_files/wsf_fact_initiatives.pdf

Women's Sports Foundation UK (2006) 'The Place of Gender Equity in Sport', www.wsf.org.uk/informed/fact_files/wsf_fact_gender.pdf

Workshops

• Women's Sports Foundation:

– WSF Women, Get Set, Go! (a sport leadership access programme)

Sexuality

DCMS (2005) 'Transsexual People and Sport – Guidance for Sporting Bodies', www.uksport.gov.uk/assets/File/Generic_Template_Documents/Publications/Standards_in_Sports_Publications/transsexuals.pdf

Stonewall (2004) 'The Employment Equality (Sexual Orientation) Regulations Guidelines for Employers', www.stonewall.org.uk/documents/employer_english.pdf

Stonewall (2004) 'Transgender (2004)', www.stonewall.org.uk/documents/BB_Trangender_Booklet.pdf

Stonewall (2006) 'Tuned Out: The BBC's Portrayal of Lesbian and Gay People', www.stonewall.org.uk/documents/tuned_out_pdf.pdf

Age

Long, J. (2004) 'Sport and the Ageing Population: Do Older People have a Place in Driving up Participation in Sport?', www.sportdevelopment.org.uk/dupageing2004.pdf

Nicholson, L. (2004) 'Older People, Sport and Physical Activity: A Review of Key Issues', www.sportscotland.org.uk/ChannelNavigation/Resource+Library/Publications/Older+People+Sport+and+Physical+Activity.htm

Sport England (2006) 'Understanding Participation in Sport: What determines sports participation among recently retired people?', www.sportengland.org/recently_retired_full_report_january_2006.doc

Miscellaneous

Boocock, S. (2002) 'The Child Protection in Sport Unit', *Journal of Sexual Aggression* (special issue on sexual harassment and abuse in sport), 8: 99–106

Child Protection in Sport Unit (2006) 'Strategy for Safeguarding Children and Young People in Sport 2006-2012' www.thecpsu.org.uk/Documents/SafeguardingStrategy.pdf

Department for Culture, Media and Sport (2000) 'A sporting future for all', www.sportdevelopment.org.uk/html/sportfutureforall.html

Equality Standard (2004) 'The Equality Standard. A Framework for Sport', www.brassingtonweb2.co.uk/content/showcontent.aspx?contentid=220

Equality Standard (2006) 'Scottish Governing Body Support for the Preliminary Level of the Equity Standard', www.brassingtonweb2.co.uk/vagacms/eqscotland2.aspx

Hayes, S and Stidder, G (2003) Equity and Inclusion in Physical Education. Leeds: Coachwise Business Solutions. ISBN: 978-0-415282-25-3.

Kirby, S. and Wintrup, G. (2002) 'Running the gauntlet in sport: An examination of initiation/hazing and sexual abuse', *Journal of Sexual Aggression* (special issue on sexual harassment and abuse in sport), 8:. 49–68.

Slinn, N. (2006) *Safeguarding and Protecting Children: a guide for sportspeople*. Leeds: Coachwise Business Solutions. ISBN: 978-0-905540-26-6.

Sneyd, S. (2006) How to Coach Sports Safely. Leeds: Coachwise Business Solutions. ISBN: 978-1-902523-50-4.

sports coach UK (2004) 'Sports Coaching in the UK', www.sportscoachuk.org/research/Research+Publications/Sports+Coaching+in+the+UK.htm

sports coach UK (2005) *Code of Practice for Sports Coaches* (leaflet). Leeds: Coachwise Business Solutions

Sport England (1999) 'The Value of Sport', www.sportengland.org/bestval.pdf

Sport England (2000) 'Making English Sport Inclusive: Equity Guidelines for Governing Bodies', www.sportengland.org/equity.pdf

Sport England (2002) 'Access for Disabled People', www.sportengland.org/disabled.pdf

Sport England (2002) 'Participation in Sport in England: Sports Equity Index 2002', www.sportengland.org/sporting_equity_2002.pdf

Sport England (2004) 'The National Framework for Sport in England', www.sportengland.org/national-framework-for-sport.pdf

Sport England (2006) 'Health and Safety: Hazards, Risk Assessments, Method Statements and COSHH', www.sportengland.org/02_hazards_ras_mss_coshh.pdf

Sport England (2006) 'No Limits: Sport England's Equity Policy', www.sportengland.org/sportsequity_policy.pdf

Sport England (2006) 'Physical Activity and Sport playing it's part in delivering Choosing Health', www.sportengland.org/physical_activity_resource.pdf

Sport England (no date) 'Response by Sport England to Consultation White Paper on Fairness for All: A New Commission for Equality and Human Rights', www.sportengland.org/cehr_-_se_response.pdf

sportscotland (2003) 'Ethics in Sport',
www.sportscotland.org.uk/ChannelNavigation/Our+activities/TopicNavigation/Ethics/

Workshops

• **sports coach UK**:

– Coaching and the Law

– Equity in Your Coaching

– Safeguarding and Protecting Children

• running**sports**:

– A Club for All – attracting more members from the community

© *Action Images/Reuters*

8.2 sports coach UK Contacts

sports coach UK
114 Cardigan Road
Headingley
Leeds LS6 3BJ
Tel: 0113-274 4802
Fax: 0113-275 5019
Email: coaching@sportscoachuk.org
Website: www.sportscoachuk.org

sports coach UK works closely with sports governing bodies and other partners to provide a comprehensive service for coaches throughout the UK. This includes an extensive programme of workshops, which have proved valuable to coaches from all types of sports and every level of experience.

For further details of sports coach UK workshops in your area, contact the sports coach UK Workshop Booking Centre:

sports coach UK Workshop Booking Centre
Tel: 0845-601 3054
Email: scukworkshops@sportscoachuk.org
Website: www.sportscoachuk.org/sports+coach+UK+Events+and+Courses/
sports+coach+UK+Workshops/

Details of all sports coach UK publications are available from:

Coachwise 1st4sport
Chelsea Close
Off Amberley Road
Armley
Leeds LS12 4HP
Tel: 0113-201 5555
Fax: 0113-231 9606
Email: enquiries@1st4sport.com
Website: www.1st4sport.com

Appendix A
Terminology Associated with Sports Equity

Term	Definition
Bisexual	People who emxperience sexual attraction toward, and responsiveness to, both males and females; a bisexual person.
Disadvantage	As a result of discrimination (see definition below), some groups are deprived of all or some resources.
Discrimination	The action people take on the basis of their prejudices. Discrimination occurs when a prejudiced person has the power to put their prejudices into action, which results in unfair and unjust treatment. **Direct discrimination** occurs when someone is treated worse than other people in the same or a similar situation. **Indirect discrimination** occurs when there is a rule or condition that applies to everybody, but people from a certain group are not able to meet it and there is no justifiable reason for having that rule.
Empowerment	Providing people with the knowledge, information and skills to enable them to have more control over decisions that affect their lives.
Ethnic group	Distinct groups identifiable by a combination of factors, including race, common nationality, traits, customs, culture and traditions[1].
Ethnic minority	An ethnic group within a society or region that is smaller in numbers than the majority population. A minority population is often a subordinate group of people, whose group members have significantly less control or power over their lives than members of a dominant or majority group[2].
Gay	Males who experience a sexual attraction toward, and responsiveness to, other males; a homosexual male.
Gender equality	Equal status, rights and responsibility for men and women.
Harassment	Harassment is described as inappropriate actions, behaviour, comments or physical contact that is objectionable or causes offence to the recipient. It may be directed towards people because of their gender, appearance, race, colour, ethnic origin, nationality, age, sexual preference, a disability, or some other characteristic.
Homophobia	The irrational fear of homosexuals, homosexuality, or any behaviour, belief, or attitude of self or others, which doesn't conform to rigid sex-role stereotypes. It is the fear that enforces sexism and heterosexism.

[1] and [2] Definition from *Clean Bowl Racism: A Report on Racial Equality in Cricket*. Reproduced with the kind permission of the ECB Racism Study Group.

Term	Definition
Institutional racism	The Macpherson Report[1] defines institutional racism as: *The collective failure of an organisation to provide an appropriate and professional service to people because of their colour, culture or ethnic origin. It can be seen or detected in processes, attitudes and behaviour which amount to discrimination through unwitting prejudice, ignorance, thoughtlessness and racist stereotyping which disadvantage minority ethnic people.* This definition can be applied to all disadvantaged groups who are discriminated against.
Lesbian	Females who experience a sexual attraction toward, and responsiveness to, other females; a homosexual female.
Positive action	Enabling employers and organisations to afford and encourage access to facilities, services, training or employment opportunities. For example, a governing body of sport may feel that a particular group of people is under-represented among its registered coaches. It decides to train more coaches and ensures that coaches from the under-represented groups are included in their plans[2].
Positive discrimination	Arising when a disadvantaged individual or group is singled out and treated more favourably than others. Positive discrimination is illegal. For example, a governing body of sport may feel that a particular group of people is under-represented among its registered coaches. Positive discrimination would occur if the governing body of sport proceeded to appoint people from this group without considering others, who were better qualified.
Prejudice	Describing negative feelings, thoughts and attitudes people have about other people that have no rational basis. Often ill-considered or pre-conceived and show bias towards certain groups of people. Everyone has prejudices about all kinds of things (eg food, clothes).

[1] Macpherson, W. (1999) *The Stephen Lawrence Inquiry: Report of an Inquiry by Sir William Macpherson of Cluny.* London: The Stationery Office. Cm 4262-I

[2] Based on a definition from *Tackling Racism in Your Sport* (Novlette Rennie, 24/25 November 1999).

Term	Definition
Race	A group of individuals within a biological species. Groups of humans with distinct physical characteristics, such as skin colour and physical features[1].
Racial discrimination	There are three main types of unlawful racial discrimination[2]: • **Direct discrimination**: when someone is treated worse on racial grounds than other people in the same or a similar situation. • **Indirect discrimination**: when there is a rule or condition that applies to everybody, but people from a certain racial group are not able to meet it and there is no justifiable reason for having that rule. • **Victimisation**: when someone may be targeted for making a complaint under the Race Relations Act 1976.
Racial equality	Equal status, rights and responsibilities for people of different racial groups.
Stereotyping	Grouping or labelling people because they share a particular trait(s), which is regarded as characteristic of that group. Stereotyping is usually negative and is frequently used to justify discrimination.
Transgender	Transsexual people have the deep conviction that the gender to which they were assigned at birth on the basis of their physical anatomy (referred to as their 'birth gender') is incorrect. That conviction will often lead them to take steps to present themselves to the world as the opposite gender. Often, transsexual people will undergo hormonal or surgical treatment to bring their physical identity into line with their preferred gender identity (referred to in this guidance as their 'acquired gender').
Victimisation	Victimisation is defined as when someone is treated less favourably than others because he or she has taken action against an organisation under one of the relevant Acts/Regulations (as previously outlined) or provided information about discrimination, harassment or inappropriate behaviour.

[1] Definition from *Clean Bowl Racism: A Report on Racial Equality in Cricket*. Reproduced with the kind permission of the ECB Racism Study Group.

[2] Commission for Racial Equality (1998) *Racial Discrimination is Against the Law – Campaign to Increase Young People's Awareness of Their Rights Under the Race Relations Act*. Campaigns Pack. London: Commission for Racial Equality.

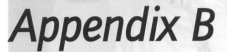

Appendix B

Organisations and Equity Initiatives

The government has recognised the value of sport in promoting the inclusion of all groups of people in society, and as part of programmes to reduce crime and antisocial behaviour. The government agenda in relation to equity in society in general also applies to sport. As a result, many initiatives and organisations have been introduced to improve the sporting opportunities available to the key target groups. This appendix provides a summary of the key organisations and initiatives you should be aware of. It is divided into the following four sections:

- Government Agenda takes a look at key government initiatives designed to provide better sporting opportunities for disabled people, people from ethnic minorities and women and girls.
- Sports Agenda examines the progress made by key UK sports organisations.
- Coaching Agenda looks at coaching-specific initiatives.
- Equality Agenda looks at equality agendas across the UK.

This appendix will help you look at the *bigger picture* beyond government policy and understand why sports equity in coaching is so important.

Government Agenda

A Sporting Future for All (2000)

In April 2000, the government launched a new sports strategy entitled A Sporting Future for All. This strategy seeks to give a lead in creating a more coordinated approach to improving sporting opportunities for all sections of the community and improving performance in international competitions. More specifically, it aims to improve the opportunities for disabled people, people from ethnic minorities and girls and women to participate, lead, coach and officiate in sport.

Coaches have a central role to play in A Sporting Future for All. The strategy aims to ensure that coaches of sufficient quality and quantity are available from the grass roots of sport to the international arena.

A Sporting Future for All can be viewed online at the Department for Culture, Media and Sport's (DCMS) website: www.culture.gov.uk

Policy Action Team 10 (PAT 10): A Report to the Social Exclusion Unit (1999)

Policy Action Team 10 (PAT 10): A Report to the Social Exclusion Unit recommends that sport be used as part of programmes to reduce crime and antisocial behaviour. It also highlights the need for an increase in the number of people from disadvantaged groups taking part in sport. This can only happen if sport is seen by these groups to be equitable and available to them.

PAT 10: A Report to the Social Exclusion Unit can be viewed online at the Department for Culture, Media and Sport's (DCMS) website: www.culture.gov.uk

Social Inclusion – Opening the Door to a Better Scotland (1999)

This report, published by the Scottish Office in 1999, highlights the potential role of sport in promoting social inclusion. The Scottish Executive's aim is to increase participation in sport by people at all age and ability levels, and to encourage young people to remain active in sport as they enter and progress through adulthood. Through **sport**scotland, the Scottish Executive will encourage improved access to sport by promoting equality of opportunity, whether the inequality is linked to poverty, geographical isolation, race or gender discrimination or disability.

Social Inclusion – Opening the Door to a Better Scotland can be viewed online at The Scottish Executive's website: www.scotland.gov.uk

The Macpherson Report (1999)

This is the report of the Stephen Lawrence inquiry. The report found that institutional racism played a part in the flawed investigation by the Metropolitan Police into the murder of Stephen Lawrence. The Macpherson Report defines institutional racism as:

...the collective failure of an organisation to provide an appropriate and professional service to people because of their colour, culture or ethnic origin. It can be seen or detected in processes, attitudes and behaviour which amount to discrimination through unwitting prejudice, ignorance, thoughtlessness and racist stereotyping which disadvantage minority ethnic people.

The Macpherson Report (1999)[1]

As a result of the Macpherson Report and recommendations made by the Commission for Racial Equality, the Race Relations (Amendment) Act 2000 was introduced to extend the Race Relations Act 1976 to a wide range of public authorities (see page 98 for further information).

Copies of the Macpherson Report are available from The Stationery Office

[1] Macpherson, W (1999) *The Stephen Lawrence Inquiry: Report of an Inquiry by Sir William Macpherson of Cluny*. London, The Stationery Office. Cm 4262-I

The Brighton Declaration (1994)

The first international conference on women and sport took place in Brighton in 1994. Aimed at decision-makers from governmental and non-governmental sectors, it focused entirely on women and sport. There were three main outcomes from the conference:

- an International Strategy on Women and Sport
- the Brighton Declaration
- the creation of the International Working Group on Women and Sport (IWG).

The Brighton Declaration is addressed to all governments and organisations that are responsible for, or have some influence over, women in sport. It complements all other laws, charters, codes and rules relating to women and/or sport and provides a comprehensive set of principles for the development of opportunities for women and sport. Its overriding aim is:

...to develop a sporting culture that enables and values the full involvement of women in every aspect of sport.

Women and sport and the challenge of change (Sport England, 1994)

The Brighton Declaration can be viewed online at the IWG's website: www.iwg-gti.org

Game Plan: A Strategy for Delivering Government's Sport and Physical Activity Objectives

Published in December 2002, this comprehensive document was produced jointly by the government's Strategy Unit and the Department for Culture, Media and Sport.

With sections that include comparative participation and sports performance data, research statistics and theories underpinning the value of sport (such as they are), it details the government's vision and strategy for sport from both a mass participation and performance perspective up until 2020.

This document was published prior to the awarding of the 2012 Olympic Games to London.

Game Plan was larger and more comprehensive than any other recent 'sport policy' documents, and sought to provide statistics and comment about sport participation and the inequalities associated with it, to provide a rationale for plans to reduce these inequalities.

It also attempted to provide both a rationale and action plan for the development of sport itself, and the reduction of social exclusion, by providing opportunities in sport participation, based largely on the claims made for sport in the report of the social exclusion unit's Policy Action Team 10. Game Plan made suggestions toward sport being a potential instrument in achieving the government's wider sociopolitical agenda of combating social exclusion.

Game Plan articulated a clear statement that government perceived sport and physical activity as a potential social instrument, to reduce the inequalities of opportunities for people (citizens) to participate in the social structures of British society.

Game Plan can be viewed online at:
www.cabinetoffice.gov.uk/strategy/downloads/work_areas/sport/sport.pdf

Every Child Matters

Every Child Matters is the government's scheme outlining five outcomes that are key to well-being in childhood and later life. They are:

- being healthy
- staying safe
- enjoying and achieving
- making a positive contribution
- achieving economic well-being.

The government's aim is to improve on these outcomes for all children.

Every Child Matters can be viewed online at: www.iwg-gti.org

Sports Agenda

Equality Standard for Sport

The Equality Standard for Sport (the Standard) is a framework and vehicle for widening access and increasing the participation and involvement in sport and physical activity of under-represented individuals, groups and communities, especially women and girls, ethnic minority groups and disabled people. It will assist sports organisations in developing equality-proofed policies, structures and processes, and will allow for performance to be assessed, thus ensuring continuous improvement in equality.

The Standard is a collaboration of the four home country sports councils and UK Sport, and is supported by the Central Council of Physical Recreation (CCPR), the Women's Sports Foundation, the English Federation of Disability Sport and Sporting Equals. Progress through the Standard is a mandatory condition within the national funding agreements involving Sport England, governing bodies of sport, and national and regional sports organisations in England. For those governing bodies of sport with a UK-wide remit, UK Sport has linked the achievement of each level within the Standard with models of good governance, as outlined in Investing in Change.

The Standard Explained

The Standard is based on two broad areas of activity:

• **Developing Your Organisation**

This will be a reflection of the culture, policies, leadership and people.

• **Developing Your Services**

This refers to the impact that policies, leadership and people have on an organisation's programmes, communications and customer service. It encompasses the four levels of achievement: Foundation, Preliminary, Intermediate and Advanced.

Foundation

The organisation is committed to equality and that commitment is communicated to all staff and volunteers.

Preliminary

The organisation is clear about what it needs to do to achieve equality, it understands the issues and barriers faced by under-represented groups in sport, and has a robust equality action plan that all staff, volunteers and key stakeholders understand.

Intermediate

The organisation is increasing opportunities for participation and involvement by a diverse range of people, including representation of its own leadership, staff, board and senior volunteers. All internal policies pay due regard to diversity.

Advanced

Leadership and staff (including coaches and officials), as well as participants, are offered a fair and equal opportunity, and are reflective of the community the organisation serves. Equality is central to the way an organisation carries out all of its work. All affiliated organisations and clubs are able to engage and develop participants, coaches, officials and administrators from under-represented groups.

Assessment and Verification of Achievements

In order to make progress through the Equality Standard for Sport, organisations will have to provide, for each level, a portfolio to evidence achievements. Portfolios will then be assessed and verified by panels employed and convened by relevant sports councils.

Sports Council Equity Group

Sports equity is coordinated on a UK-wide basis through the Sports Council Equity Group. This group is made up of UK Sport and the four home country sports councils. The purpose of this group is to:

• work more collaboratively across the UK (between sports councils)

• widen the equality agenda

• ensure training takes place in the area of equality

• annually set dates in advance for effective meetings.

The terms of reference for the Sports Council Equity Group are to:

• agree work priorities in all areas of equity and inclusion across the UK

• work collaboratively to influence the sports agenda in the UK

• promote consistency in implementing collaborative or common projects

• share expertise, good practice and relevant experience

• lead the strategic development and implementation of the Equality Standard

• engage and consult with relevant agencies to ensure effective implementation of equity and inclusion in the UK.

The Sports Council Equity Group Model

England

NI

Scotland

Wales

Strategy

Policy

Implementation

**HCSC / UK Sport
(Hosts and (Chair)
Minutes)**

Officers Groups

DECISION

Every two
months
Papers in
advance

Extends
to include

2 per (1 Seminar)
year

Sporting
Equals

WSF

**EQUALITY ADVISORY
MEETING**

ADVICE AND
SUPPORT

UK Disability
CEOs

Anti-sectarianism

CCPR Sports
Forums

Stonewall

Government
Agencies

Community
Relations

HCSC
Appropriate
Officers(eg
Women's
Officers)

Sport England

3rd Floor, Victoria House
Bloomsbury Square
London
WC1B 4SE
Tel: 0845-8508 508
Fax: 020-7383 5740
Email: info@sportengland.org
Website: www.sportengland.org

Sport England's aim is to create an active nation through sport, working to sustain and increase participation in community sport. It is the government's community sport key delivery partner in England and a Lottery distributor.

It does this through investing in sport and the sports infrastructure, providing support and advice to national and regional partners across the country, and promoting sport and its benefits.

Its investment supports facilities development, ensuring that the infrastructure is in place to deliver community sport to more people. Alongside this work to ensure people have places to play sport, it also invests in the people that make sport happen on the ground – encouraging, developing and supporting clubs, coaches and volunteers through the Delivery System for Sport in England.

Sport England has a specific focus on priority groups who are currently under-represented in sport, including women and girls, disabled people, those from black and ethnic minority and deprived socioeconomic groups. Improving equality of access to sport, and the need to address existing barriers to sport, is central to Sport England's work.

Sport England facilitates community-based opportunities for children, young people and adults of all ages (especially those within hard-to-reach priority groups). It also ensures all its national partners have equity policies and plans in place and its regional sports boards (RSBs) consider the impact of proposed projects on priority groups when making community investment decisions. Sport England is driving the roll-out of the Equality Standard and itself became one of the first organisations to achieve both the Foundation and Preliminary Levels in early 2006.

Sport England can provide the following support:

• advice on increasing participation, regionally and nationally

• equity guidelines and resources

• investment in the Sports Equity Alliance

• research into levels of participation and barriers to participation

• investment in running**sports**, the package of training and development resources for sports volunteers.

sportscotland

Caledonia House, South Gyle
Edinburgh EH12 9DQ
Tel: 0131-317 7200
Fax: 0131-317 7202
Email: library@sportscotland.org.uk
Website: www.sportscotland.org.uk

A Vision for Equity in Scottish Sport

The vision for Scottish sport is for Scotland to be a country:

• where sport is more widely available to all

• where sporting talent is recognised and nurtured

• that achieves and sustains world-class performance in sport.

At the core of this vision, is the principle of sport for all. That means that all Scottish residents, regardless of ability, ethnic group, gender, age, background, sexuality and marital or civil partnership status, should have equal opportunities, not only to participate in sport recreationally, but also to develop talent and to achieve excellence.

Underpinning the vision to transform Scotland into a truly sporting nation, as set out in the national strategy for sport, are the dual challenges of increasing participation and improving performance. Rising to meet these challenges will be critical to the successful achievement of the vision for Scottish sport.

One of the key aims of **sport**scotland's corporate plan is to increase participation in Scottish sport. To help achieve this aim, **sport**scotland has identified the need to work with its partners to increase participation by people from a number of target groups, including:

– women and girls

– disabled people

– people from ethnic minorities.

sportscotland's Work on Equity

sportscotland published its **Single Equity Scheme** ('the Scheme') on 4 December 2006. The Scheme is an integrated strategy and action plan, which sets out **sport**scotland's planned work in equity over the period from December 2006 to December 2009. It sets out how **sport**scotland will fulfil its public-sector duties to promote disability equality, race equality and gender equality, as placed upon **sport**scotland by the Disability Discrimination Act 2004, Race Relations (Amendment) Act 2000 and the Equality Act 2006 respectively.

sportscotland, in partnership with the other sports councils in the UK, is committed to the roll-out of the **Equality Standard: A Framework for Sport** ('the Standard'). **sport**scotland achieved Foundation level of the Equality Standard in June 2006, and supported 12 pilot Scottish governing bodies (SGBs) towards achievement of the Standard during 2005–2007. **sport**scotland remains committed to supporting the SGBs to achieve the Standard, and to achieving further levels of the Standard itself.

sportscotland is also very active in terms of work in relation to specific equity areas. It works in close partnership with Scottish Disability Sport to develop disability sport in Scotland, and with the Women's Sport Foundation to develop sport and physical recreation for women and girls.

In addition, it has also produced a brochure that provides an overview of the key areas of ethics in sport. This 'Ethics in Sport' brochure can be accessed by visiting www.sportscotland.org.uk/ethics (the website also contains a wealth of information about ethics in sport and, more specifically, equity).

Sports Council for Northern Ireland

House of Sport
Upper Malone Road
Belfast BT9 5LA
Tel: 028-9038 1222
Fax: 028-9068 2757
Email: info@sportni.net
Website: www.sportni.net

The Sports Council for Northern Ireland (SCNI) is committed to providing equality of opportunity for everyone who wishes to participate in sport to the level of their choice and with due regard to the need to promote equality of opportunity between:

• persons of different religious belief, political opinion, racial background, age, marital status or sexual orientation

• men and women generally

• persons with a disability and persons without

• persons with dependants and persons without.

SCNI will continue to examine ways of increasing opportunities for people who are under-represented in sport to access opportunities to take part in sport to the level of their choice. It reviews and screens all policies and programmes to ensure equality of opportunity for all, in accordance with Section 75 of the Northern Ireland Act 1998.

In working towards achieving this objective, SCNI has:

• developed and adopted a Sports Equity Policy and a Disability Mainstreaming Policy

• developed a range of sports equity courses and resources designed to support sports clubs and organisations in working towards equality

• played a role in the development and implementation of the UK Equality Standard for Sport.

Sports Council for Wales

Sophia Gardens
Cardiff CF11 9SW
Tel: 0845-045 0904
Fax: 029-2030 0600
Email: scw@scw.co.uk
Website: www.sports-council-wales.co.uk

The Sports Council for Wales is committed to the promotion of equity and diversity and works to ensure that all people and all communities have access to sport.

Child Protection and Equity

The Sports Council for Wales has in place a dedicated child protection and equity officer. Part of this role is to implement, monitor and evaluate ethics and equity policies and practices within Welsh governing bodies of sport.

Equality Standard

The Sports Council for Wales forms a key part of the Sports Council Equity Group (SCEG), which consists of a representative from each home country. SCEG works to develop a coordinated approach to equality across sports councils in the UK. The group have developed the Equality Standard for Sport, which is the first of its kind. The Equality Standard has been developed to widen access and reduce inequalities in sport and physical exercise.

In addition to the overarching equity work carried out by the Sports Council for Wales, there are a number of specific projects and initiatives developed and supported by the council to target under-represented groups in sport.

Women and Girls

A women and girls sport forum has been established since 2001 and meets regularly across the country. This allows the Sports Council for Wales to report on progress being made and to advise on how it can improve its programmes, and influence its partners and the existing infrastructure of sport to respond to the needs of women and girls.

Disability

The Federation of Disability Sport Wales (FDSW) works alongside the Sports Council for Wales in a joint commitment to the provision of high-quality education and training for coaches and volunteers working within disability sport. This continued development of inclusive coach education leads to increased sporting opportunities for all individuals, regardless of their disability status.

Young People

Through the Active Young People programmes, the Sports Council for Wales has invested in developing young people's participation and will create long-term cultural change and lifelong habits leading to health gains, as well as increasing participation in sport. Young people have been the focus of much of the work of the Sports Council for Wales for many years.

Ethnic Minority Groups

All the Sports Council for Wales' programmes offer the opportunity for all communities to overcome the barriers affecting participation in sport and physical activity. These are magnified in areas where there are large ethnic minority communities. Corporately, the Sports Council for Wales has put in place the Race Equality Scheme, which is supported by a yearly action plan. On the ground, officers' are striving to create stronger links with ethnic minority communities through engagement, representation and communication.

Socially Disadvantaged Groups

Many areas of Wales are characterised by large pockets of social and economic deprivation. Sport and physical activity have a key role to play in promoting better health, social inclusion and community cohesion in these areas. A fundamental aim of the Sports Council for Wales Active Communities project is to invest in Wales' most recreationally and socioeconomically deprived communities and Communities First areas to develop sport and physical activity participation and support community regeneration.

UK Sport

40 Bernard Street
London WC1N 1ST
Tel: 020-7211 5100
Fax: 020-7211 5246
Email: info@uksport.gov.uk
Website: www.uksport.gov.uk

UK Sport aims to promote the highest standards of sporting conduct and explore its wider social applications.

Initiatives include working with athletes, officials and key partners to promote the highest standards of conduct and fair play, both on and off the field of play. In addition, UK Sport takes a leading role in promoting equality in sport to ensure there are no barriers to participation and involvement in the running of sport for any social groups.

The overall aim is to support the development of a fair, equitable and ethical world-class sporting system in the UK that is athlete-centred and people-focused.

UK Sport embraces the spirit of all equality legislation and is committed to eradicating any form of unfair discrimination. UK Sport will not tolerate discrimination, either directly or indirectly, on the grounds of race, disability, class or social background, religious belief, sexual orientation, ethnic or national origins, gender, marital or parental status, pregnancy, age, colour or political persuasion.

UK Sport is committed to achieving equality in sport and is taking a proactive approach in this area. It is a central principle of a dynamic and modern sports organisation that can demonstrate democratic governance with progressive strategies and programmes.

To underline its commitment, UK Sport leads on the following:

• Women and Leadership Development Programme – UK Sport is committed to gender equality in sport and recognises that the situation for women in leadership is such that positive action is required. The programme provides training and support for women with the talent and desire to achieve senior positions in sport. The programme not only reaffirms UK Sport's commitment to gender equality, but also contributes to worldwide impact goals in terms of international representation and advancing world-class standards, by improving governance in sport.

• The Equality Standard: A Framework for Sport – the Equality Standard is a framework to guide sport and community organisations towards achieving equality. It will assist organisations in developing structures and processes, assessing performance and ensuring continuous improvement in equality.

• Paralympic World Class Pathway – this supports Paralympic athletes through the three key levels of the pathway: World Class Talent, Development and Podium.

• Ethical research – one element of UK Sport's 100% ME programme is ethical research into attitudes surrounding doping. UK Sport has previously carried out research into ethics in sport, primarily focused on fair play at high-profile events.

Sports Equity Alliance in England

The Sports Equity Alliance brings together a unique association of partners to promote equity within sport, and to develop cross-cutting work to achieve equality for women and girls, people with disabilities and people from ethnic minorities.

The Sports Equity Alliance also recognises the impact of social exclusion on participation in sport.

Background

- In 2005–06, Sport England commissioned a review of its three equity partners: the Women's Sports Foundation, the English Federation of Disability Sport and Sporting Equals.
- This review created the Sports Equity Alliance – an umbrella organisation representing the three equity partners and other organisations interested in promoting equality within sport.

Mission

- The Sports Equity Alliance unites the leading independent sports equity agencies in England in their efforts to achieve equality within sport.

The Sports Equity Goal

- The Sports Equity Alliance will promote and guide work to achieve the sports equity goal – to sustain and increase participation (playing, administrating, coaching, managing and officiating) in sport and physical activity among those who are under-represented in sport, through changing the culture of sports organisations at a national, regional and local level.

The Role of the Sports Equity Alliance

- Acting as one voice on collaborative work in relation to sports equity.
- Providing the first point of contact in matters relating to sports equity and signposting enquiries appropriately.
- Managing and developing collaborative working.
- Raising the profile of equity and acting as advocates of, and for, sports equity.
- Shaping and monitoring the effectiveness of cross-cutting partner work for sports equity, by raising standards in the implementation of equality initiatives.
- Influencing and advising Sport England.
- Action planning the broader agenda of sports equity.
- Collectively demonstrating and celebrating success.
- Reporting and measuring progress against the seven key drivers.

The Seven Key Drivers

1. Leadership and accountability.
2. Expertise and advice.
3. Research.
4. Training and education.
5. Increasing resources for sports equity.
6. Communication and information.
7. Disability participation pathways.

For more information on the Sports Equity Alliance, please contact any of the three partners: EFDS, WSF or Sporting Equals.

Disability

Disability Sport Wales

Welsh Institute of Sport
Sophia Gardens
Cardiff CF11 9SW
Tel: 029-20665 781
Fax: 029-20665 781
Email: office@fdsw.org.uk
Website: www.disabilitysportwales.org

Disability Sport Wales embraces two new schemes:

• National Performance Scheme

• Local Development Scheme.

The schemes aim to increase participation among disabled people and improve opportunities for talented disabled competitors to fulfil their potential. They are managed by two national officers coordinated by the Federation of Sports Associations for the Disabled (FSAD) and the Sports Council for Wales.

Disability Sports Northern Ireland (NI)

Unit 10
Ormeau Business Park
8 Cromac Avenue
Belfast BT7 2JA
Tel: 028-9050 8255
Textphone: 028-9050 8254
Fax: 028-9050 8256
Email: email@dsni.co.uk
Website: www.dsni.co.uk

Disability Sports Northern Ireland (Disability Sports NI) is the national umbrella body responsible for the coordination, promotion and development of sport for disabled people throughout Northern Ireland. It has initiated and organised a range of projects and works closely with sports providers and governing bodies of sport to promote the inclusion of people with disabilities in mainstream sport.

English Federation of Disability Sport (EFDS)

Manchester Metropolitan University
Alsager Campus
Hassall Road
Alsager
Stoke-on-Trent ST7 2HL
Tel: 0161-247 5294
Minicom: 0161-247 5644
Fax: 0161-247 6895
Email: federation@efds.co.uk
Website: www.efds.net

The English Federation of Disability Sport (EFDS) is the principal national agency responsible for the coordination and development of sport for disabled people in England. Launched in 1998, EFDS operates on a national and regional basis, and has the direct support and involvement of all major disability sports organisations. The EFDS works closely with the seven national disability sport organisations, governing bodies of sport of sport, local authorities and other statutory and voluntary organisations. The EFDS also work closely with its equity partners Sporting Equals and the Women's Sports Foundation through the Sports Equity Alliance, to improve the landscape of sporting opportunity for all.

Scottish Disability Sport

Caledonia House
South Gyle
Edinburgh EH12 9DQ
Tel: 0131-317 1130
Fax: 0131-317 1075
Email: admin@scottishdisabilitysport.com
Website: www.scottishdisabilitysport.com

Scottish Disability Sport (formerly the Scottish Sports Association for Disabled People [SSAD]) was formed in 1962 to provide facilities for, and to encourage the development of, sport and physical recreation for disabled people. Scottish Disability Sport has now acted as the governing and coordinating body of all sports for all people with a disability for over 30 years.

SDS has in place a strategic plan, 'Towards London and Beyond, 2006–2012', which provides a framework for all its operations. 'Towards London and Beyond' highlights four strategic goals which influence its work. These goals will:

- support the development of a sporting pathway for young people with physical, sensory or learning disabilities
- encourage and support Scottish athletes with a disability to realise their full potential in sport
- recruit new partners involved in physical activity and/or disability and further develop existing partnerships
- work with regional coaching partnerships to access the very best of education and leadership for athletes and volunteers
- introduce individuals with disabilities to sport through local development programmes at foundation and participation level.

sportscotland invests in SDS and is proud to be a supporter of this positive and proactive organisation.

149

Ethnicity

Sporting Equals

Fairgate House
Kings Road
Tyseley
Birmingham B11 2AA
Tel: 0121-707 9340
Email: info@sportingequals.com
Website: www.sportingequals.com

Funded by Sport England, Sporting Equals is a national initiative working to promote racial equality in sport throughout England. It was established in 1998 as a partnership between Sport England and the Commission for Racial Equality and, in 2006, a separate company, Sporting Equals Limited, was created; a company that is on par with other sports equity partners.

Major initiatives launched by Sporting Equals include:

• Racial Equality Charter for Sport – a public pledge signed by the leaders of sport committing them to use their influence to create a world of sport in which all people can participate in watching, playing and managing sport, without facing racial discrimination of any kind

• Achieving Racial Equality – A Standard for Sport – a standard developed by Sporting Equals in partnership with the Commission for Racial Equality and Sport England, to help sports organisations and governing bodies of sport plan, develop, evaluate and achieve racial equality in all aspects of sport. Organisations working towards the Standard are likely to have signed up to the Racial Equality Charter for Sport (see above). The Standard covers three main areas:

    – commitment, policy and planning

    – participation and public image

    – administration and management.

There are three levels of achievement – preliminary, intermediate and advanced. Organisations are required to submit evidence of achievement in the three main areas at each level. Sporting Equals and Sport England verify the evidence and reward organisations that achieve all the objectives at each level.

Promoting Racial Equality Through Sport: A Standard for Local Authority Sport and Leisure Services ('the Standard') is designed to assist local authorities in planning, developing and promoting racial equality through the formulation and delivery of their sports provision and services. The Standard has been developed in partnership between the Local Government Association and Sporting Equals.

The Standard will bring further recognition to the value of sport in tackling issues of inequality within communities, provide a tool to assist best value and comprehensive performance assessment frameworks and help local authorities to meet the general statutory duty as outlined in the Race Relations (Amendment) Act 2000.

Sport for Communities

Sport for Communities is a national initiative managed by Sporting Equals and funded for three years by the Invest to Save Budget programme, which is sponsored by the Department for Culture, Media and Sport (DCMS).

It aims to support the development of integrated sporting activities in inner-city communities, particularly targeted at people from ethnic minorities, refugee and migrant backgrounds. To enhance this, employment opportunities in sport will be developed with these communities.

The project will be managed by Sporting Equals and delivered in partnership with two main groups of agencies that have a national and regional presence – the governing bodies of sport and local authority sport and leisure services. Local ethnic minority communities, refugees and migrants will also be involved and included as partners.

Women and Girls

Women's Sports Foundation (WSF)

3rd Floor, Victoria House
Bloomsbury Square
London WC1B 4SE
Tel: 020-7273 1740
Fax: 020-7273 1981
Email: info@wsf.org.uk
Website: www.wsf.org.uk

The Women's Sports Foundation (WSF) is the only organisation in the UK that is solely committed to promoting and improving opportunities in sport for women and girls, at every level. The WSF works to create a positive environment in which women and girls from different cultural, social and religious backgrounds have an equal opportunity and adequate resources to be involved in an activity of their choice, at their chosen level and capacity.

Priorities of the WSF include promoting women and girls' participation in all aspects of sport and physical activity, celebrating and promoting women's sporting success, and equality for women working in the sport and leisure industry. The WSF works closely with its equity partners, Sporting Equals and the English Federation of Disability Sport through the Sports Equity Alliance, to improve the landscape of sporting opportunity for all. It also runs its own initiatives in partnership with other organisations, to encourage and support women to become involved in coaching.

Sexuality

Stonewall

Stonewall Equality Limited
Tower Building
York Road
London SE1 7NX
Telephone: 020-7593 1850
Fax: 020-7593 1877
Email: info@stonewall.org.uk
Website: www.stonewall.org.uk

Stonewall was founded in 1989 by a small group of women and men who had been active in the struggle against Section 28 of the Local Government Act.

The aim from the outset was to create a professional lobbying group that would prevent such attacks on lesbians, gay men and bisexuals from ever occurring again. Stonewall has subsequently put the case for equality on the mainstream political agenda, by winning support within all the main political parties, and now has offices in England, Scotland and Wales.

Stonewall is renowned for its campaigning and lobbying. Some major successes include helping achieve the equalisation of the age of consent, lifting the ban on lesbians and gay men serving in the military, securing legislation allowing same-sex couples to adopt, and the repeal of Section 28. More recently, Stonewall has helped secure civil partnerships and ensured the Equality Act 2006 protected lesbians and gay men in terms of goods and services.

The Gender Trust

PO Box 3192
Brighton BN1 3WR
Helpline: 07000-790 347
Contact: 01273-234 024
Email: info@gendertrust.org.uk
Website: www.gendertrust.org.uk

The Gender Trust is the only registered charity in a position to help adults in the UK who are transsexual, gender dysphoric, transgender (ie those who seek to adjust their lives to live as women or men, or come to terms with their situation despite their genetic background), or those whose lives are affected by gender identity issues.

The Gender Trust mission is:

...to improve the quality of life of trans people and their families, by supporting them and working with anyone who is affected by gender identity issues.

Its vision is:

...that everyone will accept and support the right of trans people to be valued members of society.

Age

Age Concern

Astral House
1268 London Road
London SW16 4ER
Free helpline: 0800-00 99 66
Website: www.ageconcern.org.uk/

Its underlying principles are as follows:

• Ageism is unacceptable – it is against all forms of unfair discrimination, and challenges unfair treatment on grounds of age.

• All people have the right to make decisions about their lives – it helps older people to discover and exercise these rights.

• People less able to help themselves should be offered support – it seeks to support older people to live their lives with dignity.

• Diversity is valued in all that it does – it recognises the diversity of older people and their different needs, choices, cultures and values.

• It is only through working together that it can use its local, regional and national presence to the greatest effect.

Its work is also guided by the following set of values:

• Enabling – it enables older people to live independently and exercise choice.

• Influential – it draws strength from the voices of older people, and ensures that those voices are heard.

• Dynamic – it is innovative and driven by results and constantly delivers for older people.

• Caring – it is passionate about what it does and cares about each individual.

• Expert – it is authoritative, trusted and quality-oriented.

Corporate Priorities 2007–2010

• To prevent poverty and maximise income in retirement.

• To promote age equality and enable older people to make full contributions to our economy, society and neighbourhoods.

• To maximise healthy life expectancy and promote health, independence and well-being for all older people.

• To achieve greater social inclusion of the most disadvantaged older people and challenge the causes of exclusion.

• To achieve a step change in effectiveness and efficiency, in which a crucial element will be a greater focus on older people as customers and contributors to all that we do.

Child Protection in Sport Unit

NSPCC National Training Centre
3 Gilmour Close
Beaumont Leys
Leicester LE4 1EZ
Tel: 0116-234 7278
Fax: 0116-234 0464
Email: cpsu@nspcc.org.uk
Website: www.thecpsu.org.uk

Each week, more than eight million UK children take part in sport. They do so in a range of settings, from local groups to national competitions. But while most enjoy themselves in safety, a small number are at risk of abuse from individuals who choose sports work to gain access to children. Adults working in sport are also in a unique position to identify and act on concerns for children that arise outside the sporting environment.

The National Society for the Prevention of Cruelty to Children (NSPCC) works with the UK's sport councils, governing bodies and other organisations to help minimise the risk of child abuse during sporting activities.

Central to this work is the Child Protection in Sport Unit (CPSU), which was founded in 2001 as a partnership between the NSPCC and Sport England. The Unit's role is to:

• be the first point of contact for sports organisations regarding safeguarding and child protection issues and individuals after sports organisations

• coordinate the production of child protection information and training for sports organisations

• commission research into a range of issues relating to child protection in sport

• develop and promote standards for safeguarding and child protection procedures and training in all sports.

Coaching Agenda

sports coach UK

114 Cardigan Road
Headingley
Leeds LS6 3BJ
Tel: 0113-274 4802
Fax: 0113-275 5019
Email: coaching@sportscoachuk.org
Website: www.sportscoachuk.org

sports coach UK is the only organisation in the UK that is dedicated to the development of coaching and coaches. sports coach UK believes that the composition of the coaching community should reflect that of the broader community, in terms of gender, ethnic origin and ability. However, it recognises and acknowledges that disabled people, people from ethnic minorities and women and girls are under-represented in all spheres of coaching, umpiring and officiating.

sports coach UK's equity action plan outlines the way in which the organisation intends to take positive action to increase the involvement of under-represented groups within the coaching community. It is currently implementing the plan in partnership with:

• county sport partnerships

• local authorities

• governing bodies of sport

• the five sports councils

• English Federation of Disability Sport

• Sporting Equals

• Women's Sports Foundation.

sports coach UK was one of the first organisations to be awarded the Achieving Racial Equality – A Standard for Sport at preliminary level (see page 150 for further details).

For further information about sports coach UK's equity action plan, contact the Equity Policy Development Team at the above address.

UK Coaching Framework – a 3–7–11-year action plan

The need for such a plan arises from the increasing significance to the sporting and wider government agenda of coaching in the UK. Sport has a high national profile and it is now recognised at government level throughout the UK that sport and physical activity contribute significantly to the health, social inclusion and identity of the nation. The long-term vision for sport sets out two overarching objectives to be achieved by 2020: to increase and widen the base of participation and to achieve success on the world stage.

Further development of the UK Coaching Framework (formerly the UK Action Plan for Coaching) is rapidly gathering pace in advance of the second Coaching Summit. There has been a great deal of debate and agreement regarding this document and its associated actions, which is reflected in the working practices of all those involved in implementation.

The UK Coaching Framework provides the blueprint for developing the system that will take coaching in the UK forward towards the goal of being the best in the world by 2016. The framework will ensure that both the development and delivery of the coaching system is relevant across the whole of the UK, taking into account the policies, strategies and priorities of the devolved administrations and the home country sports councils.

The UK Coaching Framework has been developed following an extensive consultation process between January and June 2006. The first draft was formally endorsed by key funding partners and home country sports councils at the UK Coaching Summit, held in Grantham on 26 and 27 April 2006, and was formally endorsed by the Sports Cabinet in January 2007.

The vision of the UK Coaching Framework is to be number one in the world by 2016, creating a cohesive, ethical, inclusive and valued coaching system where skilled coaches support children, players and athletes at all stages of their development in sport.

Building towards this vision, the UK Coaching Framework will be implemented in three main phases:

Building the Foundations (2006–2008 – three years)
Delivering the Goals (2006–2012 – seven years)
Transforming the System (2010–2016 – 11 years)

Five strategic action areas, underpinned by 12 specific actions, have been identified:

A. The UK Coaching System

Action 1: The UK coaching model – Develop a UK coaching model that will provide a clear direction and strategic framework for coaching policy and practice in the UK.

Action 2: Participant pathways – Set out and implement a clear, comprehensive and inclusive model for the long-term development of sports participants across the UK.

Action 3: Coach pathways – Set out and implement a clear, comprehensive and inclusive model for the long-term development of coaches across the UK.

Action 4: Coaching strategies – Set out and implement sport-specific coaching strategies at UK, national, regional and local levels.

B. Front-line Coaching

Action 5: Active and qualified coaches – Recruit and retain qualified coaches with the skills to coach inclusively at each phase of the player pathway.

Action 6: Coaching in education – Maximise the role of coaching in the education sector.

C. Support for Coaches

Action 7: Coaching support and system delivery – Establish effective education, delivery systems and resources to support the development of coaches and the coach education workforce in the context of the UK Coaching Certificate and effective CPD programmes.

Action 8: Targeted development of coaches – Establish appropriate systems to identify, train, qualify and support high-quality coaches for specific populations within sport: commencing with coaches of high-performance athletes, talent-identified athletes, children and including coaches of disabled people.

Action 9: Specialist qualifications and CPD – Develop specialist qualifications in coaching, linked to pathway phase/target group/disability and commencing with the inclusive coaching of primary-age children as a first step.

D. Professionally Regulated Vocation

Action 10: Licensing and registration – Set out and implement the steps needed to establish coaching as a professionally regulated vocation which is open to all, recognising volunteer, part-time and full-time roles. As a first step, conduct a detailed feasibility study on the licensing and registration of coaches.

Action 11: Profile and recognition of coaching – Conduct a sustained campaign to maximise the profile and recognition of coaching at all levels.

E. Research and development

Action 12: Research and development – Implement an ongoing research and development programme into athlete and coach pathways and coaching interventions, in line with the priorities of the Coaching Framework.

(See the UK Coaching Framework section at www.sportscoachuk.org)

Governing Bodies of Sport

All sports have a governing body that has a responsibility for the development, regulation and ethical framework of the sport it governs. As part of this responsibility, sports have developed ethical frameworks for child protection and drug and doping abuse, as well as for sports equity.

Governing bodies of sport in receipt of funding from any of the sports councils will have a sport equity/equality policy in place and will be working towards a level within the equality standards, as described on pages 138 and 139. In some cases, they will have a dedicated officer to support the development of sports equity.

Equality Agenda

The Commission for Equality and Human Rights (CEHR)

Kingsgate House
66–74 Victoria Street
London SW1E 6SW
General enquiries: 020-7215 8415
Email: info@cehr.org.uk
Website: www.cehr.org.uk

The new Commission will be a non-departmental public body (NDPB) and independent influential champion, whose purpose will be to reduce inequality, eliminate discrimination, strengthen good relations between people and protect human rights.

The CEHR will take an active role in helping to achieve change to benefit some of the most vulnerable and least well represented people in our society.

The CEHR will bring together the work of the three existing Commissions: the Commission for Racial Equality (CRE), Disability Rights Commission (DRC) and Equal Opportunities Commission (EOC).

Equal Opportunities Commission

England
Arndale House
Arndale Centre
Manchester M4 3EQ
Tel: 0845-601 5901
Fax: 0161-838 8312
Email: info@eoc.org.uk
Website: www.eoc.org.uk

36 Broadway
London SW1H 0BH
Tel: 020-7222 1110
Fax: 020-7222 2771
Email: info@eoc.org.uk

Scotland
St Stephens House
279 Bath Street
Glasgow G2 4JL
Tel: 0845-601 5901
Fax: 0141-248 5834
Email: scotland@eoc.org.uk

Wales
Windsor House
Windsor Lane
Cardiff CF10 3GE
Tel: 0845-601 5901
Fax: 029-2064 1079
Email: wales@eoc.org.uk

The Equal Opportunities Commission deals with sex discrimination and inequality related to gender, including good practice in the fair and equal treatment of men and women.

Equality Commission for Northern Ireland

Equality House
7–9 Shaftesbury Square
Belfast BT2 7DP
Tel: 028-90 500 600
Textphone: 028-90 500 589
Enquiry Line: 028-90 890 890
Fax: 028-90 248 687
Email: information@equalityni.org

The Equality Commission for Northern Ireland is an independent public body established under the Northern Ireland Act 1998. The Commission's duties and functions are set out in the legislation for which they have responsibility. General duties include:

• working towards the elimination of discrimination
• promoting equality of opportunity and encouraging good practice
• promoting affirmative/positive action
• promoting good relations between people of different racial groups
• overseeing the implementation and effectiveness of the statutory duty on public authorities
• keeping the relevant legislation under review.

Disability Rights Commission

DRC Helpline
Freepost MID02164
Stratford upon Avon CV37 9BR
Tel: 08457-622 633
Textphone: 08457-622 644
Fax: 08457-778 878

The Disability Rights Commission (DRC) is an independent body established in April 2000 by Act of Parliament to stop discrimination and promote equality of opportunity for disabled people.

Commission for Racial Equality

St Dunstan's House
201–211 Borough High Street
London SE1 1GZ
Tel: 020-7939 0000
Fax: 020-7939 0001
Email: info@cre.gov.uk

Scotland (Edinburgh)
The Tun
12 Jackson's Entry (off Holyrood Road)
Edinburgh EH8 8PJ
Tel: 0131-524 2000
Fax: 0131-524 2001
Textphone: 0131-524 2018
Email: scotland@cre.gov.uk

Wales (Cardiff)
3rd Floor
Capital Tower
Greyfriars Road
Cardiff CF10 3AG
Tel: 02920-729 200
Fax 02920-729 220
Email: InformationWales@cre.gov.uk

The CRE works for a just and integrated society, where diversity is valued. They use persuasion and their powers under the law to give everyone an equal chance to live free from fear of discrimination, prejudice and racism.

Appendix C

Religious Festivals

It may not be appropriate for people to take part in sport during important religious festivals. The table below lists the main festivals celebrated by people from different religions. You should always take these into account when scheduling coaching sessions, events or competitions. The dates of the festivals may vary from year to year, so you are advised to consult the *Shap Calendar of Religious Festivals*[1] for details of dates in particular years.

The list is by no means exhaustive, so remember to consult with individual participants too.

Name of Festival	Religion	Description
Christmas Day	Christian	A major festival in the Christian faith, which celebrates the birth of Jesus, who Christians believe to be the Son of God. Gifts are reminders of the offerings brought to the infant Jesus.
Easter Day	Christian	The most important festival of the Christian year, when Christians celebrate the resurrection of Jesus. Easter eggs are given, which symbolise new life.
Eid ul-Fitr	Muslim	A three-day festival of the breaking of the fast, which comes at the end of Ramadan and at the start of the first of Shawwal, the tenth month of the Muslim calendar. It is a time for almsgiving, new clothes, good food, presents for children, family get-togethers and contact with friends. The community assembles for Eid prayer at the mosque or another suitable venue.
Hanamatsuri	Japanese and Buddhist	A flower festival marking the Japanese celebration of the Buddha Shakyamuni's birthday. The flowers accentuate the tradition that the Buddha was born in a garden, so floral shrines are made and an image of the infant Buddha is set in it and bathed.
Navaratri/Durga Puja/Dusserah	Hindu	One of the few festivals celebrated across India. Navaratri means nine nights, which is how long the festival lasts. The final three days are the most important.

[1] Available from the Shap Working Party on World Religions in Education.

161

Name of Festival	Religion	Description
Passover/Pesach	Jewish	A major eight-day festival when Jews commemorate the Exodus from their slavery in Egypt. A highlight is the Seder meal held in each family's home at the beginning of the festival, when the story of their deliverance is recounted. Matzah (unleavened bread) is eaten throughout the festival, as are other foods that contain no leaven.
Ramadan	Muslim	The month of fasting from dawn to sunset. To the Muslim, fasting means abstaining from all food, drink, smoking and marital relations during daylight hours. It is an exercise in self-discipline and enables everyone to have some experience of deprivation. The fast is traditionally broken each evening by taking dates and water. Children may be encouraged to fast, although the full fast is not compulsory until maturity.
Yom Kippur	Jewish	The final day of the ten days of repentance. It is the holiest day of the year in the Jewish calendar. The Bible calls it the Sabbath of Sabbaths and it is marked by afflicting the soul – expressed through a total fast lasting 25 hours. Jews spend most of the eve and most of the day in prayer.

New Year Festivals

Some of the New Year festivals celebrated by people from different religions are listed below:

- Al-Hijra (Muslim)
- Chaitra (Hindu)
- Divali/Deepavali (Hindu)
- Ethiopian New Year's Day (Rastafarian)
- Ganjitsu (Japanese)
- Rosh Hashana (Jewish)
- Vaisakhi (Baisakhi) (Sikh)
- Yuan Tan (Chinese).

This list is not exhaustive, so remember to consult with individual participants too.

The text in this appendix is based on information from the Shap Calendar of Religious Festivals. Reproduced with the kind permission of the Shap Working Party on World Religions in Education.

Appendix D

Useful Suggestions for Working with Disabled People

Most people want to treat disabled employees, job applicants and customers the same way as everyone else, but aren't always sure how to go about it. These suggestions aren't part of the Disability Discrimination Act 1995 and 2004, but they may be useful when you meet disabled people.

Remember!

- Disabled people are individuals just like everybody else. Don't make assumptions about their abilities or their needs. Don't forget that some impairments are hidden (eg epilepsy and mental illness).

- If you aren't sure how something might affect a disabled person, ask her for advice.

Communication

- If a disabled person is with someone, talk to the disabled person directly, not to the person who is with him. This also applies to a deaf person accompanied by a sign language interpreter.

- When talking to a deaf person, find out (if necessary, in writing) whether she lip-reads. If she does:
  - make sure your face is in the light
  - look directly at the person
  - speak clearly and naturally
  - remember to keep your hands away from your face.

- When you first meet a blind person, introduce yourself. When you are going to move away, tell him. Don't leave him talking to an empty space.

- When you are talking to someone with a speech impairment, concentrate on what is being said, be patient and don't try to guess what she wants to say. If you don't understand, don't pretend you do.

- If someone has difficulty understanding you (perhaps because they have a learning disability), be patient and be prepared to explain something more than once. Concentrate on using simple language.

- When talking to a wheelchair user, try to ensure that your eyes are at the same level as his, perhaps by sitting down. Don't lean on the wheelchair — it is part of the user's personal space.

- Avoid asking personal questions about a person's impairment, such as 'Were you born like that?' But an employer could ask 'Does your disability affect your ability to do this job?'

- If someone looks different, avoid staring. Concentrate on what she is saying, not on the way she looks.

- If you are talking to an adult, treat him like an adult.

Assistance

- If someone looks as if she needs assistance, offer it, but wait for her to accept before you help.

- When guiding a blind person, do not push or pull him. Ask if he would like to take hold of your arm. If there are any steps, tell him whether the steps go up or down.

- Remember that guide dogs for blind people, hearing dogs for deaf people and other assistance dogs are working dogs, not pets. They should not be fed, patted or distracted when they are working.

- Above all, put yourself in the disabled person's place. Most of the above points are just good manners.

Language

Some of the words and phrases we use offend disabled people, because they suggest that the disabled person is dependent or helpless. Some words, such as cripple or retarded, have become terms of abuse or are used to make fun of disabled people. Below are some common words to avoid, with suggested alternatives:

- Do not say *the disabled*, use *disabled people*.
- Do not say *suffering from, crippled by, afflicted by* or *a victim of*, use *a person who has* or *a person with*.
- Do not say *deaf and dumb*, use *deaf without speech*.
- Do not say *an epileptic*, use *a person with epilepsy*.
- Do not say *spastic*, use *a person with cerebral palsy*.
- Do not say *mentally handicapped* or *subnormal*, use *a person with a learning disability*.
- Do not say *confined to a wheelchair* or *wheelchair bound*, use *wheelchair user*.

The text above and on the preceding pages is based on information from DL200 (guidelines issued on behalf of the Minister for Disabled People. Prepared in conjunction with the National Disability Council and RADAR.). Reproduced with the kind permission of RADAR.

Coaching People with Learning Disabilities

- Be patient, tolerant, consistent and tactful, but ensure that participants understand the boundaries of acceptable behaviour.
- Break down complex skills into smaller steps.
- Establish the level to which instructions and directions are understood.
- Avoid using abstract models.
- Enable simple decision making.
- Avoid drills that rely heavily on numeracy and literacy skills.
- Coach by showing and copying, not telling.
- Be aware that the motor skills and physical fitness of some participants may be generally poor due to lack of opportunities to participate in sporting activities, or even take regular day-to-day exercise.

Appendix E

Glossary of Racial Terms

African	A native inhabitant of the continent of Africa. A person of African descent or ancestry. Africans are generally divided into North Africans (north of the Sahara desert) and Sub-Saharan Africans (south of the Sahara desert). Sub-Saharan Africans are generally, but not always, very dark-skinned compared to the lighter-skinned northern Africans.
Asian	A native inhabitant of the continent of Asia. A person of Asian descent or ancestry. Asians are generally divided into South Asians, who are mainly of Indian origin, and Orientals, who are mainly of Chinese and Japanese origin. South Asians are generally, but not always, dark-skinned.
Black-British	In its widest sense, a non-white citizen of Great Britain, including Asians and Orientals. Also used to describe non-white/non-English British inhabitants, who were born in Britain. In its narrowest sense, refers to British-born British citizens of African or Caribbean descent.
British-born African	A person of African descent or ancestry born in Great Britain.
British-born Asian	A person of Asian descent or ancestry born in Great Britain.
British-born Black	Non-white, British-born British citizens. In its narrowest sense, refers to British-born British citizens of African or Caribbean descent.
British-born Caribbean	A person of Caribbean descent or ancestry born in Great Britain.
Caribbean	A native inhabitant of the Caribbean. The majority population of the Caribbean is dark-skinned, made up of peoples of African, South Indian and Oriental ancestry. Caucasian (white) persons are prevalent.
Country of birth	The actual country where an individual was born. Country of birth is distinct from nationality or ethnicity.
Country of origin	The birthplace of a person and/or parents and, in some instances, grandparents.
Culture	The customary beliefs, social forms and material traits of racial, ethnic, religious, or social groups. Socially patterned human thought and behaviour. Culture is social heritage or tradition that is passed on to future generations. It is shared, learned human behaviour – a way of life.
Customs	Habitual course of action, usual behaviour and a particular established way of behaving.
Ethnic	Relates to races or large groups of people classed according to common nationality, traits, customs, culture and traditions. Ethnicity is more likely to denote origin or birth than political nationality.

Ethnic groups	Distinct groups identifiable by a combination of factors, including race, common nationality, traits, customs, culture and traditions.
Ethnic minority	An ethnic group within a society or region that is smaller in numbers than the majority population. A minority population is often a subordinate group of people whose group members have significantly less control or power over their lives than members of a dominant or majority group.
Ethnic origin	One's parentage and ancestry (racial and geographical).
Ethnicity	Ethnicity has to do with group identification. When we talk of ethnicity, we indicate that groups and identities have developed in mutual contact, rather than in isolation.
Mixed race/bi-racial/ dual heritage	The offspring of a union between persons of different races.
Multicultural	Reflecting more than one cultural group; diverse cultures.
Plural society	A form of society embracing many majority groups and cultural traditions.
Race	A group of individuals within a biological species. Groups of humans with distinct physical characteristics, such as skin colour and physical features.
Race relations	Inter-racial/ethnic connections, usually for the promotion and maintenance of mutual interest, involvement and benefits of all the groups concerned.
Racial	Concerning groups of individuals identifiable or differentiated by race.
Racialism	Discriminatory actions resulting from racist beliefs.
Racism	Conduct, words or practices which advantage or disadvantage people because of their colour, culture, or ethnic origin.
Racist	One who believes that populations should be categorised based on physical genetic features; that some races or ethnic groups are superior to others; that inferior groups should not have the same basic human rights as their superiors.
South Asian	A native inhabitant or descendent of southern Asia, including India, Pakistan, Bangladesh and Sri Lanka. South Asians are generally, but not always, dark-skinned.
Tradition	An inherited, established, or customary pattern of thought or action. Beliefs and customs handed down, generally by word of mouth, or by behaviour.
West Indian	A native inhabitant of one of the Caribbean islands, which were formerly British colonies, known as the *West Indian* islands, together with British Guyana and British Honduras. The majority population of the (former) West Indian islands is dark-skinned, made up of peoples of African, South Indian and Oriental ancestry. Caucasian (white) persons are prevalent in most of the islands.

White English	The indigenous population of England (and Wales).
White race	White-skinned or light-skinned race of people, most often Europeans. The white race is also known as *Caucasian*.
White-other	The minority white population in England, usually not English born, or second-generation whites.

Definitions adapted from Clean Bowl Racism: A Report on Racial Equality in Cricket. Reproduced with the kind permission of the ECB Racism Study Group.

Appendix F

Levels of Participation for Disabled Participants

The model in Figure 1 will help you understand the opportunities available to disabled participants.

Figure 1: The Winnick Model

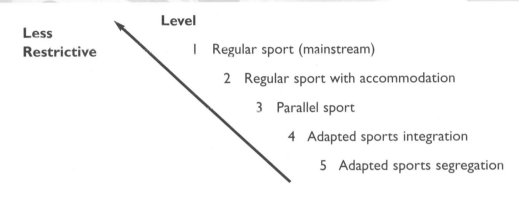

Adapted from Winnick, P.J. (1987) 'An Integration Continuum for Sports Participation', *Physical Activity Quarterly*, Vol 4 (3): 158.

This model was developed by Winnick in 1987 to show the different levels at which disabled participants could train and compete.

Level 1: Regular sport (mainstream)

Total integration (coaching, competition and social) of disabled participants into mainstream competition and clubs (eg an athlete with a learning disability training, competing and socialising in a local athletics club).

Level 2: Regular sport with accommodation

Integration of disabled participants into regular competition, clubs and coaching, with some flexibility in the rules and regulations to enable integration and equal opportunities with non-disabled peers (eg wheelchair tennis players and non-disabled tennis players playing up and down doubles, where wheelchair players are allowed two bounces of the ball).

Level 3: Parallel sport

Disabled participants competing in the same event as their non-disabled peers, but in their own section (eg wheelchair athletes in a marathon).

Level 4: Adapted sports integration

Disabled and non-disabled participants taking part in an adapted sport, in a segregated setting (eg forming teams for the purposes of developing a wheelchair basketball competition).

Level 5: Adapted sports segregation

Disabled participants competing in a competition solely for that particular disability group (eg goalball[1]).

---

[1] Goalball is an indoor ball game that is played by visually impaired people on a tactile court, using a ball with a bell in it.

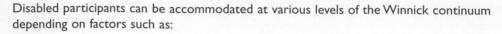

Disabled participants can be accommodated at various levels of the Winnick continuum depending on factors such as:

- individual choice
- level of ability
- type of sport
- opportunities available to the participant.

Participants could also be at different levels in Winnick's continuum for different purposes. For example, they might:

- compete at Level 1 locally, but aim for elite competition at Level 5
- train at Level 1, but compete at Levels 3 and 5
- compete at Levels 1 or 2 in one sport and Levels 3 or 5 in another
- compete at Level 5 and coach at Levels 1 and 5.

Segregation, Integration and Inclusion

To what extent should disabled participants be *integrated* into mainstream sport and when should they be *segregated*? This is a difficult question because you need to weigh up a number of issues, such as the:

- type of sport – some sports are readily accessible and individual, so integration is relatively easy (eg archery, swimming)
- views of the disabled participant – some prefer to train and compete only with other disabled participants; others prefer to be fully integrated
- views of the coach – his/her ability and willingness to adapt and organise sessions appropriately to facilitate integration
- views of other participants – they may feel they are not getting sufficient attention or their training needs are not being fully met, if programmes have been adapted to allow disabled participants to be fully integrated
- views of others – such as parents and helpers who may question the appropriateness of integrating a disabled participant into the session.

Appendix G

Participant's Questionnaire

On reflection in the last month, did your coach:

• give you attention?	not at all	hardly ever	occasionally	often	a great deal
• give you an opportunity to make your own decisions?	not at all	hardly ever	occasionally	often	a great deal
• establish a good climate in training?	not at all	hardly ever	occasionally	often	a great deal
• spend time discussing goals and priorities?	not at all	hardly ever	occasionally	often	a great deal
• encourage you to take responsibility for yourself?	not at all	hardly ever	occasionally	often	a great deal
• positively receive your ideas and act on them?	not at all	hardly ever	occasionally	often	a great deal
• take an interest in your life outside sport?	not at all	hardly ever	occasionally	often	a great deal

On reflection, in the last month how often did you feel:

• like giving up your sport?	not at all	hardly ever	occasionally	often	a great deal
• disenchanted with training/your sport?	not at all	hardly ever	occasionally	often	a great deal
• valued by your coach?	not at all	hardly ever	occasionally	often	a great deal
• highly committed to your training and sport?	not at all	hardly ever	occasionally	often	a great deal

Appendix H

Action Plan Templates

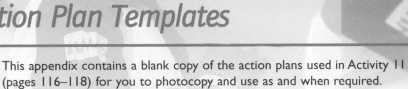

This appendix contains a blank copy of the action plans used in Activity 11 (pages 116–118) for you to photocopy and use as and when required.

SHORT-TERM IMPROVEMENTS/CHANGES

	What?	How?	When?
1			
2			
3			

LONG-TERM IMPROVEMENTS/CHANGES

What?	How?	When?
1		
2		
3		

Notes: